変化する英語
Variation and Change in Contemporary English

中尾俊夫 著

児馬修・寺島廸子 編

damn young

It's this
simple

He's done it
two days ago

ひつじ書房

略語表

A	Adjective	形容詞
Acc	Accusative	対格
Adj	Adjective	形容詞
Adv	Adverb	副詞
AE	American English	アメリカ英語
AustE	Australian English	オーストラリア英語
Aux	Auxiliary verb	助動詞
BE	British English	イギリス英語
c	century	世紀
C	Consonant	子音
Ch	Chinese	中国語
D	Dative	与格
E	English	英語
EModE	Early Modern English	初期近代英語
Esk	Eskimo	エスキモー語
EstE	Estuary English	エスチュアリ英語
F	French	フランス語
F	Female	女性
Fmn	Feminine	女性(言語上の)
G	German	ドイツ語
Gk	Greek	ギリシャ語
H	Head	主要部
Inf	Infinitive	不定詞
Int	Interjection	間投詞
IrE	Irish English	アイルランド英語

It	Italian	イタリア語
Jap	Japanese	日本語
L	Lateral	側音
L	Latin	ラテン語
M	Male	男性
ME	Middle English	中英語
Msc	Masculine	男性（言語上の）
N	Nasal	鼻音
N	Noun	名詞
Neut	Neuter	中性
Nom	Nominative	主格
Norw	Norwegian	ノルウェー語
NP	Noun Phrase	名詞句
NYC	New York City	ニューヨーク市
OE	Old English	古英語
ON	Old Norse	古ノルド語
P	Preposition	前置詞
PE	Present-day English	現代英語
Pl	Plural	複数
PP	Prepositional Phrase	前置詞句
Pron	Pronoun	代名詞
prp	present participle	現在分詞
ptp	past participle	過去分詞
RP	Received Pronunciation	容認発音
Rus	Russian	ロシア語
ScE	Scottish English, Scots	スコットランド英語
Sg	Singular	単数
Sp	Spanish	スペイン語

Sw	Swedish	スウェーデン語
UM	Unmarked	無標
V	Verb	動詞
V	Vowel	母音
VI	Intransitive Verb	自動詞
VT	Transitive Verb	他動詞
Yid	Yiddish	イディッシュ

目　次

略語表 …………………………………………………………………………ⅰ
1　はじめに……………………………………………………………………1
　1.1　変化の要因……………………………………………………………2
　1.2　変化を捉える方法……………………………………………………3

2　名詞…………………………………………………………………………5
　2.1　形容詞用法……………………………………………………………5
　2.2　複数形…………………………………………………………………5
　2.3　普通名詞化……………………………………………………………6
　2.4　所有格(属格)…………………………………………………………8
　2.5　性(gender) ……………………………………………………………11
　2.6　派生名詞 ……………………………………………………………13
　2.7　名詞化 ………………………………………………………………13

3　代名詞 ……………………………………………………………………15
　3.1　人称代名詞 …………………………………………………………15
　3.2　不定代名詞 …………………………………………………………16
　3.3　指示代名詞 …………………………………………………………18
　3.4　疑問代名詞・疑問詞 ………………………………………………18
　3.5　関係詞(relative pronoun) …………………………………………20
　　3.5.1　関係詞の選択とパラミター ……………………………………20
　　3.5.2　関係詞の選択 ……………………………………………………23
　　3.5.3　関係詞について注意すべきこと ………………………………25

4 冠詞 ……………………………………………………………29
    4.1 冠詞の交替 ……………………………………………29
    4.2 the と both …………………………………………30
    4.3 副詞の最上級と the ………………………………30

5 形容詞 …………………………………………………………31
    5.1 形容詞と節 ……………………………………………31
    5.2 形容詞化 ………………………………………………32
    5.3 a-形容詞の限定用法 …………………………………33
    5.4 比較 ……………………………………………………33

6 副詞 ……………………………………………………………35
    6.1 否定 ……………………………………………………35
    6.2 平坦副詞(flat adverb) ………………………………39
    6.3 強調詞(intensifier) …………………………………40
    6.4 文副詞の発達 …………………………………………41
    6.5 so ………………………………………………………42
    6.6 副詞化 …………………………………………………42
        6.6.1 接続詞の副詞化 …………………………………42
        6.6.2 その他の副詞化 …………………………………43
    6.7 注意すべきその他の副詞 ……………………………44

7 前置詞 …………………………………………………………47
    7.1 前置詞の交替 …………………………………………47
    7.2 前置詞の残留(p-stranding) …………………………49
        7.2.1 PP からの取り出し ……………………………49
        7.2.2 2重前置詞構造 …………………………………50
    7.3 前置詞化 ………………………………………………51

  7.4　問題のある前置詞 …………………………………………52

8　接続詞 ……………………………………………………………55

9　動詞 ………………………………………………………………57
  9.1　時制 …………………………………………………………57
  9.2　進行形 ………………………………………………………60
  9.3　受身 …………………………………………………………62
  9.4　仮定法 ………………………………………………………64
  9.5　自動詞〜他動詞 ……………………………………………67
    9.5.1　他動詞化 ……………………………………………69
    9.5.2　自動詞化 ……………………………………………75
    9.5.3　能格動詞(ergative verb)・中間動詞(middle verb) ………76

10　省略 ……………………………………………………………79
  10.1　代名詞・名詞の省略 ………………………………………79
  10.2　動詞・助動詞の省略 ………………………………………81
  10.3　接続詞の省略 ………………………………………………83
  10.4　前置詞の省略 ………………………………………………88
  10.5　冠詞の省略 …………………………………………………93

11　一致 ……………………………………………………………95
  11.1　主語と動詞の一致 …………………………………………95
  11.2　呼応 …………………………………………………………97
  11.3　kind / sort と this / that …………………………………98

12　語順 ……………………………………………………………99
  12.1　従節の中の倒置 ……………………………………………99

13	語形		101
	13.1	名詞	101
	13.2	形容詞/副詞	102
	13.3	動詞	103

14	語彙			105
	14.1	語彙		105
	14.2	借入		106
	14.3	造語		111
	14.4	転換		112
	14.5	派生(derivation)		115
		14.5.1	接辞	116
			14.5.1.1 接尾辞(suffix)	116
			14.5.1.2 接頭辞(prefix)	119
		14.5.2	結合形(combining form)	120
	14.6	逆形成(back formation)		122
	14.7	複合(compounding)		123
		14.7.1	名詞複合語	124
		14.7.2	形容詞複合語	125
		14.7.3	動詞複合語	126
		14.7.4	その他	127
	14.8	短化(abbreviation)		127
	14.9	アクロニム(acronym)		128
	14.10	混成(portmanteau)		129
	14.11	語彙の意味		129

15	発音		131
	15.1	概論	131

15.2　/ C / ……………………………………………………132
　　15.3　/ V / ……………………………………………………136
　　15.4　綴字発音 ………………………………………………144
　　15.5　アクセント ……………………………………………146
　　　　15.5.1　揺れている項目 ……………………………146
　　　　15.5.2　リアルタイムの資料 ………………………150

16　性差(sexism) ……………………………………………………153
　　16.1　差別語 ……………………………………………………153
　　16.2　男・女性語と意味 ……………………………………157
　　16.3　職業と男女差(アメリカ) ……………………………159
　　16.4　男・女ことばのちがい ………………………………159

17　婉曲(euphemism) ………………………………………………163

18　誓い(swearing)・罵倒 …………………………………………167

19　丁重さ(politeness) ……………………………………………171

20　呼び掛け・名前 …………………………………………………175

21　結論 ………………………………………………………………179

出典一覧 …………………………………………………………………185
参考文献 …………………………………………………………………191
索引 ………………………………………………………………………197
あとがき …………………………………………………………………205

第 1 章　はじめに

「21 世紀の英語」というとき、2001 年(俗には 2000 年)からの英語が 20 世紀の最後 2000 年(俗には 1999 年)と 1 晩で(すっかり)変わったという意味ではないことは当然である。これは自然な連続性のある変化の連続体を人為的な時間という尺度で切るための錯覚にすぎない。

21 世紀の英語がどんなものかを問うことは英語の変化について「予言する」ことに他ならない。英語の変化についての予言で有名なものに Sapir の *Language*（1921:7-8 章）がある。(1 a, b)がその予言の例である。

(1)　a.　Who(m) did you see?

　　　b.　　　　　SOD/Wells(1990)　　　Random House

　　　　roof　　u:　　u:〜ʊ　　　u:〜ʊ

　　　　soot　　ʊ　　　　　　　　ʊ〜u:

　　　　hoop　　u:　　　　　　　　u:〜ʊ

それによると(1 a)では whom が後退し、who が主流となり、(1 b)では [u:〜ʊ] の間で揺れているが [ʊ]へ収れんしていくという。彼の予言から約 80 年たったが、(1 a)の予言はおおよそ正しいといえよう。今日の英語では、ある資料によると「主格としての who は 58%、目的格としての who は 20%」あるいは「informal な英語では who が広く受け入れられている」(Quirk et al. 1985:367)という発言により裏付けられる。

一方、(1b)についてはsoot以外は彼の予測の反対方向へ進んでいるように見える。それはくちびるを丸める必要のある音を当該母音の前に置いていないことと関係があるかもしれない(*foot*/*book*)。

1.1 変化の要因

すべてのことばは時間とともに、発音、文法、語彙などの局面において変化する。これはことばの普遍的な特色である。ただし、言語には変化しない(しにくい)面とそうでない面がありうる。

ことばは変化している最中であってもコミュニケーションの手段として働く。それは個人に関係なく言語社会全体のことばが絶え間なく変化しているからである。

一般にことばの変化についての予言は、
（ⅰ）　現在進行中の変化および方向、
（ⅱ）　過去において実際に起こった歴史的変化および方向、
（ⅲ）　同系言語にみられる変化、
（ⅳ）　幼児の言語習得、
などに基づいて行われる。

ことばの変化は、まったく同じ条件が整ったからといって必ず生起するとは限らない。その意味で、ことばの変化は自然科学の法則(law)とはちがい、傾向(trend, tendency)を示すにすぎない。

結局、変化についての予言、記述などは、「ことばの変化を引き起こす要因は何か」という基本的な問題を解明する努力へ通じるものである。最近著者は下記のような「**変化の二層論**」を考えている。

（ⅰ）　浅い層の変化要因：　ことばの習得を終わってから10代前半ごろまでの子供が社会的な要因(年令、性差、階層など)によって「変異(variant－linguistic variable)」を引き起こし、社会の評価を受けたのち拡散、定着する。これを社会的要因(social factor)と呼んで

もよい。

（ⅱ）深い層の変化要因：　周囲のことばを入力として生まれつきもっている言語知識によって幼児がことばの習得をしていくとき、入力と出力の間に生じたギャップが変異となって変化へ進む。これは言語的要因(linguistic factor)と呼べるものである。変化は（ⅰ）よりも（ⅱ）の方が大きく根本的である。

6月24日(1999年)付け朝日新聞朝刊に「ら抜き」に関する文化庁の調査結果がのっていた。［来られますか、食べられますか、考えられる＞来れますか、食べれますか、考えれる：このような「ら抜きことば」は16才－19才の男62%、女52.4%、60才以上の男女共20%にみられる］。さらに、［とんでもないことでございます＞とんでもございません］のような変化も観察されるという。これらの変化は明らかに前者の要因によるものである。一方、平安朝に起こった促音化(重子音化)、たとえば「カツテ」＞ katte、「ヲヒテ(追ひて)」＞ otte などは後者の要因によるものである。後者の要因によるものはいろいろな言語の歴史にくり返し現れる普遍的な過程である。

1.2　変化を捉える方法

① 実際の時間軸(real time)にそって出発点Aから終着点Bにある形Xが到達するのを観察する。

② 見掛け時間(apparent time)による方法：　若い世代のことばAと老世代のことばBがちがっているならば、老世代のことばBを若い人の変化の出発点とする(B＞A)(青年期(adolescence)を越すと重要な変化を自分のことばに持ち込まない)。[注1]

	10才	40才	60才
⟨roof⟩	ʊ	ʊ～uː	uː

uː → ʊ (老世代→若い世代)

③ 類型変化(typological change)： ある言語の変化はそれと同じ(または類似した)過程がその言語と起源的に関係のある(あるいは無関係の)言語(群)に反映されていることがある。
④ 統一性原理(uniformity principle)： 直接観察しえない過去に働いた過程は現在進行中の過程を考察することでわかる。つまり現在は過去を反映する——今日働いている変化要因は過去に働いたものと同じ種類、規模である。
⑤ 特定言語の史的流れ(drift)——語彙拡散(lexical diffusion)： 現在進行中の変化は過去に始まったものの延長線上にあり、その集積であるから、描く軌跡は一定のチャンネル内にある。ただし、生起する変化は同じ文脈をもつ辞書項目すべてに同時に影響するとは限らない。いわゆる例外である。しかしその例外を予測することはできない。

	変化を受けるもの	例外
例　æ > æ:	mad　bad　glad	sad
	aunt　man　pass	ran
	half　ask	ash
		after

注1　逆に、若い世代→老世代(A > B)もありうる。

第2章　名詞

2.1　形容詞用法（⇒名詞の形容詞化）

　この用法は英語が得意とするところである。形容詞用法の名詞は単数が原則であったが近年複数形もみかけるようになる。

（1）　ten *five-dollar* bills

　　　some corner *grocery* store

（2）　*arms* talk ／ a *clothes* rack

　　　a new major *roads* policy ／ a new *trades* (trade) union ／ a *chemicals* (chemical) plant

　　　gentlemen friends (Sheldon *Rage* 320)

　　　a huge *electronics* plant (Sheldon *Sands* 352)

　　　your civil *rights* record (Sheldon *Sands* 352)

2.2　複数形

（1）分節的複数形

　① 主語の数に呼応する。

　　　she shakes her *head* ／ they shake their *heads*

(lose his *life* / lose their *lives*)

(make a *fool* of / make *fools* of)

② 必ず複数にする。

$\left\{\begin{array}{l}\text{cross}\\ \text{change}\\ \text{exchange}\\ \text{switch}\end{array}\right\}$ hands, cars / gears〜gear

③ イディオムのときは単数にする。

be on our guard / speak through the nose / lift a finger / keep an eye on / (they need) a haircut / (they lose) a leg to stand on

(2) be all N

数えられない名詞は単数形、数えられる名詞のときは複数形。all が省かれることもある。

be all anxiety / He was all muscle / be (all) sympathy

be all ears

all she saw were smiles and friendly faces（Sheldon *Bloodline* 347）

2.3 普通名詞化

最近の英語ではこれまで数えられない名詞と考えられたものの普通名詞化を、「不特定」の意味のとき a / an を用いることによって、または複数化してしばしば使う。形容詞がつくと特にそうである。不定冠詞付きにはあまり抵抗がないようにみえる。「不可算名詞に不定冠詞や複数語尾は付かない」という原則がくずれつつあるようだ。

名詞の複数化はアメリカ英語の特色。valves（valve（BE））/ e-mails / homeworks など。

（1）複数形

in our *breaths* / use your *imaginations* / *angers* / *nonsenses* /

knowledges / a variety of other *businesses* / there are *misunderstandings, jealousies*, small *hurts* / devote all his *energies*

the *snows* of February　　　　　　　　　(Sheldon *Rage* 259)

two *tears*... escaped from her brimming eyes　(Steele *Ghost* 137)

（2）不定冠詞付き

That's *a nonsense*. (1970年以後のBEの変化) / hold *a* great *love* / hold *a hatred* / with *a* quick *intelligence* and *a* strong *will* / what *a* wonderful *future* / *a power* that controlled the lives of many people / sip *a* bitter *coffee* / being with her is *a warmth, a celebration* of life / she was enchanted after *a rain* /

there is $\begin{cases} a\ dependability\ /\ a\ maturity\ /\ a\ sureness\ / \\ a\ confidence\ /\ an\ assurance\ /\ a\ savage\ fury \end{cases}$ about him

He had *a respect* that boardered on awe. / *a* warm July *rain* / *a* light *snow* / *a* light *rain* / have *a* graceful *elegance* / have *a* high *recommendation* / *a* warmer *climate* / feel *a closeness* to him / there was {*a silence* / *a strength*} that had not been there before / have *a* sweet and engaging *personality* / love one with *a* deep *love* / force *a calmness* into her voice / with *a* murderous *rage* / *a love* for their coming / *a* wonderful *education* / *a* long *illness* / *a wind* came out of nowhere

Brett glanced at her with *a love*　　　　(Hailey *Wheels* 506)

（3）amountを数えられる名詞とともに用いる（急速にnumberの領域に入る。AE, BE）。

the *amount* of men they have slept with

the *amount* of pills

　　cf. How *much* runners in this race?

（4）a.m.を名詞として

arrive here this *a.m.*

2.4 所有格（属格）

(1) 's をとるのは原則として生物であるが、とくに地名、場所、時を表す名詞は、話手にとって関心が強いとき 's を取る。主要部 (head) が1語のときにとくに 's、3語以上になると of が好まれる (the murder of an English tourist)。

Mary's umbrella / the dog's tail / the world's welfare / the history's lessons / the city's population / China's policy / last year's profit / the noun's plural / the word's meaning

the Roertses' annual holiday (＝Roerts 家の〜) (Archer *Steal* 97)

(2) 's と of

's と of の選択は (i) animate か否か (ii) NP の長さ (iii) 表す意味の3つの要因によってほぼ決まる。しかし例外も少なくない。

① animate か否か

	's	of
animate	○	
inanimate		○

the man's left eye のほうが the left eye of the man よりも自然。
the needle's eye よりも the eye of the needle のほうが自然。
第1の名詞が animate のとき of はふつうでない。

  Mary's car   *the car of Mary
  the cat's milk *the milk of the cat

England's history (the history of England), the train's arrival (the arrival of the train) については(1)参照。

② NP の長さ

	's	of
you	○	
John	○	
the pretty girl	○	○
the former prime minister ／ Sir William John	○	○
the only one person ＋ 関係節		○

*the car of you よりも your car の方が好まれる。
 the hat of John よりも John's hat の方が好まれる。
*the man's dog who… よりも the dog of the man who… の方が好まれる。
(you are) a friend *of the young lady*　　（Hailey *Hotel* 498）
from the outward look *of him*　　　（Hailey *Airport* 214）
　　cf. a barfly acquaintance *of Rollier's* （Hailey *Wheels* 226）

③ 意味

	's	of
同格		○
部分的		○
主格	○	
目的格		○

一般に名詞は 's, of いずれも可だが人称名詞は 's を取るのがふつうである。
the city of York（同格）
a few of the men（部分的）
Jane's arrival（主格）
removal of the paper ／ love of God（目的格）

④ その他

's と of が同一の NP 内に起こるときは前者が主格、後者が目的格。

Jim's love of his parents

her photograph of John

BE： 1) 's は大部分 animate N と起こる (my father's watch)
2) of は non-personal N と起こる (the bottom of her glass / the edge of the table)
3) 単音節の「時間」、「空間」、きまり文句で以前よりずっと 's が使われる。
at the day's end / the water's edge / the river's mouth / at death's door

⑤ 例外

love the warm smell *of him*

the utter kindness *of you*

her release (＜ release her)

her assistance (＜ assist her)

her murderer (＜ murder her)

She loved the look *of him* and the feel *of him* and the memory *of him*　　　　　　　　　　(Sheldon *Other* 260)

(3) 二重属格 (N of _'s と N of _)

N につづく NP が

① definite　② human であるとき

a work of my father's 〜 a work of my father

*a work of *a friend's*

*a window of *the room's*

③ N よりも代名詞の方がずっとふつう。

a friend of *his*

④ of のあとの NP が長いときは(2語以上)所有格はさけられる('s は短い(1語)とき)。

a friend of Mrs Fletchter / her other friend

(4) 主要部(head)と of 所有格

主要部が支配する of 句の間に別の要素 X をはさむことがある。これを許す主要部(H)はふつう出来事や状態を表す名詞で、-ion(generation), -ence(existence), -al(arrival), -ment(excitement)で終わる。

① X はしばしば「時」、「位置」を示す副詞句。HXof-句がふつうの語順だがまれに XHof-句ということもある。

a glint in his eye of...

in his eye a glint of...

the existence in Paris of...

② X ＝ 関係詞の場合

the remnant that exists in my memory of his book

③ X ＝ 述部(predicate)

the death is announced of Mr...

(5) 群属格(group genitive)

in *Paul's friend's* garage　　　　　(Robbins *Pred* 255)

their...tablecloth that had been *John's grandmother's*

(Steel *Gift* 210)

2.5 性(gender)

名詞を受ける代名詞の性に関して AE を中心に調査(1951年、1973年)したものによると、

(1) 国

America

　　　　　　文中に her などないとき： it 42%　they 29%　she 16%
　　　　　　　　　　　　　　　　　 we 11%
　　　　　　あるとき： she 75%　it 16%　we 2%
　　　　　　　　　　　 they 2%
　　the US
　　　　　　文中に her などないとき： she 41%　it 31%　they 19%
　　　　　　　　　　　　　　　　　 we 5%
　　　　　　あるとき： she 66%　they 14%　it 13%
　　　　　　　　　　　 we 3%
（2）船
　　the Queen Mary
　　　　　　文中に her などないとき： it 55%　she 43%
　　　　　　あるとき： she 80%　it 18%
（3）動物
　　dog
　　　　　　文中に his などないとき： he 88%　it 5%　she 3%
　　　　　　あるとき： he 90%　it 15%
　　cat
　　　　　　文中に his などないとき： it 46%　he 43%　she 9%
　　she よりも he が多い。一般に人間に身近だったり高等動物であるほど男性（masculine）か女性代名詞（feminine pronoun）で分けられやすい。
（4）人間
　　cousin　　　　　　　　she 98%　he 4%
　　child　解答者　男　　　he 16%　she 0%　it 2%
　　　　　解答者　女　　　he 36%　she 24%　it 3%
　　baby　　　　　　　　　it 52%　she 28%　he 21%

2.6 派生名詞

派生名詞使用の傾向が目立つ。

 closing ― closure
 method ― methodology (what ～ I used)
 medicine ― medication (Did you take ～)
 use ― usage (the proper ～ of the toy)
 expense ― expenditure

2.7 名詞化

（1） 元来の Adv を名詞化する。no place などをモデルとして。
 nowhere ＝ no place
 There was *nowhere* else to move   (Sheldon *Naked* 260)
 She had *nowhere* to go and no one to go to.
 Where, exactly, is *here*?   (Cornwell)
 Here'll do.(ここでいい)   (Hailey *Detective* 459)
 She'll be *here*―   Where is *here*?   (Parker *Vices* 204)

（2） 前置詞と here / there / where
 とくに from(ソース)to(目的)を表す前置詞と用いられる。前置詞がないと意味があいまいである。
 I drove from my home *to here* / Where are you *from*? /
 I want to know where it is *at* (*from*). / It's too bright *in here*. /
 He opened the door. '*In here.*'
 one of the phone calls...was *to here*   (Hailey *Airport* 331)
 So the learner moves *to there* [＝ a neighboring space]. *From there*, a further presentation of VOS, ..., will take the learner to the target.   (Dresher 1997:46)

See if there's a flight *out of here* tonight to Paris, please.
trace the leak *to there*

（3） 形容詞の名詞化

considerable ［＝ a good deal］（AE の口語で）

do *considerable* / a *considerable* of

He was beyond *handsome*　　　　　　　　　（Rice *Vampire* 48）

第3章　代名詞

3.1 人称代名詞

（1）It's me

口語では完全に確立している。他の代名詞へも及ぶ。

Who did it?　*Me.*（*I）

I'm older than *him.* / I suppose that's *her.* / It won't be *us.*

That must be *them.*　　　　　　　　（Archer *Matter* 200）

If anybody tells her anything, let it be *me*　（Cornwell *Body* 65）

it would be *him*　　　　　　　　　（Archer *Thieves* 279）

　cf. *Me* and Erick のような and で結ばれた構造で I の代わりに用いられる me はとくに若者の間で AE、BE とも用いられる。

（2）*myself* は他の（代）名詞といっしょに、あるいは比較構文でそれが指す I を欠いていても起こる。

John and *myself* were invited.

He invited John and *myself*.

He is a better man than *myself*.

It was carried out by Susan and *myself*.

のような I のない文は許されないという保守的な人もある。

(3) 代名詞の名詞化

  a lovelier *you* / the real *you*

  Have you figured out the real *me*! (Sheldon *Other* 132)

  Adorable *you* (Sheldon *Windmills* 405)

   cf. a rare *few* (Sheldon *Other* 242)

3.2 不定代名詞

(1) one

 ① Adj を伴って先行の名詞を指す。単数のときは必ず a(n), the, that など冠詞類を伴う。

  There are three dogs. I like a white *one*. / these green *ones*

  Not *a one* of us will ever be the same (Archer)

 ② 形容詞を伴わない the one, which ones, our ones, those ones などは 19 c〜20 c になって生まれた。these ones はさらに遅く発達した。one or two ones [= people] のような使い方も最近の発達。

  You know what *a one* she is. (口語) / He's *the one* I like to go with. / I'm *the one* in trouble. We are *the ones* in trouble. / He is not *one* to be frightened. / They are not *ones* to be frightened. / behave like *one* mad (*like *ones* mad)

  They [=expensive books]'ve never been read. Never. Not *a one*.

    (Koontz *Watchers* 373)

  Black E:

  you've never met any of'em. Not *a one*. (Dickey *Sister* 22)

  I didn't see *a one* [= the ladies he'd been talking about の 1 人]

    (Block *Topless* 17)

  I knew... that not *a one* of them would be able to eat

    (Robbins *Merchants* 10)

Polaroid photographers. I didn't turn up *a one*

(Block *Kipling* 176)

(2) certain / several / various

certain / various (AE), several (Sc, Ir, AE)、今日では BE でも用いる。

certain of his generation / speak to *various* of the members / *several* of my friends

(3) each other / one another
 ① 含まれる人数に関係なく用いられる。
 we see *each other* / *one another*
 The three were locked together in *each other*'s arms

(Hailey *Detective* 304)

 ② each は分離されるとき each...the other という。Sheldon の例は従節の other と呼応している例。
 each was determined that, in the end, he would destory *the other*

(Sheldon *Memories* 91)

 each found herself avidly studying the faces of *the others*

(Sheldon *Sand* 49)

 cf. *neither* can be ordered relative to *the other*

 ③ each's belief（まれながら）

(4) Floating
 The boys went *all* home. / We were *all* upset. / We were *neither of us* happy. / They will *each* bitterly criticize *the other*. / they're *most of them* a single color / they *two* went...

(5) a fair few / a good few ［= a considerable number］
 最近よく使われる。

(6) a lot > alot
 alot of fun（AE の informal な手紙などで）

3.3 指示代名詞

(1) this / that

A, B, C とあげた3例の順をさすとき in *this* order でなく in *that* order というのが原則である。

(2) 電話で「そちらはだれですか？」というとき

Who is *this* ? —— This is John.

(3) this / that の副詞化 (⇒ 副詞化)

3.4 疑問代名詞・疑問詞

(1) whom と who

Whom did you see? / *Who* did you see?

To *whom* did you give it?

Who did you give it to? (1969年の AE では可とする人 41%)

Who are you looking for? (すでに 1938年の AE では確立されていた)

	who	whom
1250-1500	0%	100%
1500-1570	0%	100%
1570-1640	3%	97%
1640-1710	8%	92%
17-18 c	11.8%	88.2%

PE	文語		口語	
	who	whom	who	whom
	3%	97%	54%	46%

① 口語では PE へ向けて who が増大していく。

I know *who* Jim cheated. (formal, informal いずれでもふつう)

② who は口語でふつう。また関係詞よりも疑問詞で、前置詞の目的語としてよりも直接目的として、pied-piping よりも前置詞の残留(P-stranding)として用いる方がふつう。

She began to know *who* you wanted to see.

She never knew where he was going or *with whom*.

(2) how come [= why, after all]

19世紀半ばごろから AE で始まり、のち BE へも入って確立した。つづく語順は SV。直接話法がふつうだが、最近、間接話法でも用いることがある。

How come you're a gardener? / *How come* I was drinking on the job? / *How come* A. J. asked me?

he is going to ask *how come* a nice girl like her is the registrant of trucks in New York　　　　　　　　　　(Sanders *Trial* 232)

(3) why don't you

'please' の意味で文頭、時に文末に起こる。

Why don't you come in?

Come in *why don't you*?

why don't you S　Let me buy you this one, *why don't you*?

　　　　　　　　　Grab a seat, *why don't you*?

why don't we S　*why don't we* go into my study?

　　　　　　　　　　　　　　　　　　(Koontz *Watchers* 326)

(4) How about ～

How about we refer to them as black?

　　cf. *What do you say* we get something to eat?

　　　　　　　　　　　　　　　　　　(Robbins *Lady* 310)

How about you give me my passport?　　(Crichton *Rising* 334)

How 'bout we make it to that mailbox?　　(Parker *Vices* 224)

How about I get it for the last five trucks that were up there, to be safe. (Cornwell *Unnatural* 34)

How about we go out on the town?　　(Robbins *Storyteller* 113)

How about I put on some coffee　　(Cornwell *Unnatural* 360)

　cf. *How about* over lunch?(食べながらどう?)

(Hailey *Detective* 300)

How 〔=what〕 *about* if I come over?　　(Block *Closet* 208)

How about if I pay for a tour?　　(Cornwell *Potter's* 301)

(5)　多重疑問文(multiple question)

I wonder to *whom* he said *what*. *When* will you do *what*?

I wonder whom$_i$ they think that they will meet t$_i$

I wonder whom$_i$ they ask $\begin{cases} *\text{if } [= \text{whether}] \\ *\text{whether} \\ *\text{wh-} \end{cases}$ they will meet t$_i$

adjunct clause (when, because, if などに導かれる副詞節)の中からのとり出しも不可。

*I asked whom$_i$ they will be excited {when / before} they meet t$_i$

It's not clear *who* did *what* to *whom*　　(Crichton *Disclosure* 488)

who wrote *what* about *whom* in *what*　　(Drabble *Year* 100)

3.5　関係詞(relative pronoun)

3.5.1　関係詞の選択とパラミター

　一般に wh- 関係節が that- 関係節やゼロ関係節に比べ拡大している。それは wh- が関係詞(疑問詞)のはっきりした「しるし」をもっていることによる。

	BE	AE	
	(1900-1980年)	(1987年の調査)	(1995年の調査)
wh-	66.9-90.5%	34%	35%
that	6.7-17.6%	45%	44%
ゼロ	1.5- 8%	21%	21%

(1) 直接目的格の関係詞は

		BE	AE 1995
書きことばでは	wh-	60-80%	(ただし書き・話しことば両方含む。)
	that	20%	
	ゼロ	5-9%	wh- 7%
話しことばでは	wh-	25-40%	that 46%
	that	30-50%	ゼロ 47%
	ゼロ	20-30%	

関係節の中で関係節化されやすい名詞句は、主語 > 直接目的語 > 前置詞の目的語 > 所有格（属格）名詞の順である。

(2) 生物か非生物(animacity)

[＋human] として wh- が、[－animate] では that が好まれる。ゼロはやや [＋human] が多い。

1995	wh-	that	ゼロ
＋Human	80%	23%	59%
－Anim	20%	77%	42%

(3) 文体

書きことばでは wh- が、話しことばでは that、ゼロが好まれる。

1995	wh-	that	ゼロ
話しことば	24%	68%	63%
書きことば	76%	32%	37%

(4) 関係詞と先行詞の隣接

1995	wh-	that	ゼロ
先行詞＋関係詞	42%	48%	76%
先行詞 X 関係詞	49%	58%	16%
先行詞関係詞関係詞	59%	44%	62%

ここでは関係詞の選択を問題にしている。

Something happened that I didn't count on.（先行詞 X 関係詞の例）

(5) 埋め込み節における関係節化される名詞句の位置

that / ゼロは直接(間接)目的語で好まれるが wh- は直接目的語で好まれず、主語で好まれる。

1995	wh-	that	ゼロ
主語	47%	53%	0%
直接目的語	7%	46%	47%
前置詞の目的語	41%	29%	30%
属格	100%	0%	0%

(6) 制限か非制限

（Brown Corpus による AE 1977 の調査）

	制限	非制限
which	74.75%	25.25%
that	100%	0%

BE

who... は　　　　　［＋human］［＋animate］の先行詞のとき、

that / which は　［－animate］の先行詞のとき、

that は　　　　　［＋animate］だが［－human］のとき、

　　　　　　　　　［＋human］でもクラスの代表のとき、

　　　　　　　　　［－definite］の代名詞のとき好まれる。

　cf. a baby that cries in considerable hours

3.5.2 関係詞の選択

(1) who と whom

who と whom はとくに関係詞節が you {believe / know} などの挿入節を含むとき揺れる。

Benjamin, *whom* she had been told was its producer...
women, *whom* Noelle felt were there
anyone *whom* the group thought might be interesting

不変化の who は口語で圧倒的で、関係詞よりも疑問詞として、前置詞の目的語よりも直接目的語で、また pied piping よりも P-stranding の P の目的語でふつう。P, VT の目的語でも who のときがある。

not knowing who is sitting with *who* / it was unclear who had ambushed *who*

	who	whom
a) the man＿escaped was...	100%	0%
b) the girl＿you watched eat it is...	60%	40%
c) the guy＿you met last night is...	60%	40%
d) the girl＿John said drank the wine is...	90%	10%
e) the man to＿you talked is...	0%	100%
f) the man ＿you delivered the pizza to is my brother	80%	20%

(2) of which と whose

史的には 16〜17 c の間に whose が増大、18 c に頂点に達した。しかしその後減少、PE では of which は EModE よりも少しふつうの程度。EModE 以降 of which を無生物と、whose を生物と使う傾向が増す。PE では前者は生物を指さない。whose は 18 c 以降減っていく。なお whose を「人」について使って、「物 / 動物」については使わないが 80%、使うが 20% である。

	of which	whose
1500-1570	13.3%	86.7%
1570-1640	13.8%	86.2%
1640-1710	19.3%	80.7%
1740 s	36.2%	63.8%
late 18 c	61.4%	36.4%
PE 書きことば	26.6%	73.4%
話しことば	15%	85%

BE

whose: 先行詞が inanimate, animate(人、動物)のとき。ときに that's + NP がみられる (the house *that's* roof is white)。(⇒3.5.3(11))

of which: inaminate のときは whose よりも好まれる。

（3） that と which

that は制限に使われ、which は非制限的に多く使われることの他に

the book {that / which} I read last night

の違いを調べてみると区別しない 45%、区別する 55% である。

（4） that と who

the only, the + 最上級のときでも who が多い。

Lawrence was the only one *who* seemed genuinely pleased

(Archer *Matter* 267)

He was the only one *who* was truly disappointed...

(Grisham *Runaway* 99)

3.5.3 関係詞についての注意すべきこと
（1） that と非制限用法
① A, B, C..., that や that の前位置に固有名詞が来て、それが直前の名詞と同格のとき。

There was a look about him, an air of easy confidence, *that* made her feel... （Sheldon *Naked* 17）

She was wearing a dark gray wool dress, with a little white collar and a black bow tie, *that* she had bought with her salary

（Steel *Gift* 174）

② which が期待されるとき

she smiled a funny little smile, *that* made him want to lean over and kiss her （Steel *Ghost* 319）

There was some force in her that was irresistible, *that* would obtain anything she wanted （Sheldon *Other* 111）

a black leather-bound Bible, Cambridge Red better edition, *that* she claimed to have borrowed from someone's office

（Cornwell *Unnatural* 236-7）

These things, *that* had seemed ... beyond the grasp of her imagination, were becoming familiar to her. （Drabble *Waterfall* 143）

the two hotels, in Moblile and Charleston, *that* were losing so much money （Archer *K & A* 308）

we will then be served the most magnificient langouste you have ever tasted, *of that* I can assure you （Archer *Hiccup* 126）

（2） 二重制限の関係節（double relative）

2つめ以下の関係節は最初の関係節を含む先行文全体を先行詞とする (that)... {that / who} 制限用法。

There was not one single thing *that* she needed *that* she did not have （Sheldon *Stranger* 309-10）

He was the only man φ I've ever known *who* was totally without compassion (Sheldon *Morning* 46)

(3) 疑問詞を先行詞とする関係節

必ずしも that が好まれておらず who がみられる。

Who was it *who* had said...? (Sheldon *Stranger* 136)

(4) 関係節と分裂文

it is...{who / that} がふつうで whose はきわめてまれ。

It is Mary *whose* address I lost.

(5) than whom

idiomatic で than を P のように扱って今日なお文語で使われる。

 cf. better than *me*

She would have had a lot to say about whether or not I liked you, *who* you were prettier *than*, and... (Steel *Gift* 108)

(6) 文頭の which

とくに AE で時折みかける。必ずしも文語調とは限らない。

"That's the kind of singer I want to become." *Which* is pretty much what she wanted when she was there.

'I—I need more muslin.' *Which* was the last thing she needed.

(Sheldon *Sands* 125)

(7) PE では関係節にあたる内容をドイツ語のように複合形容詞として表すことがしばしばある。

an off-the-record comment

a once-in-a-lifetime experience

(8) 再叙代名詞(resumptive pronoun)

questions, *some of which*, had *they* been put to her in the privacy of her own home, she would have found objectionable

(Archer *Prod* 295)

your *permission, which* if we don't get *it*, the next step'd be a count order

(Block *Williams* 347)

Which, if anyone noticed *it*, he could blame on Falstaff

(Koontz *Moon* 361)

(9) every which way

idiom で 'in all directions, in a disorderly manner' の意味。

最初 AE、のち BE でも用いられる。

people running *every which way*

(10) 代名詞を先行詞とする非制限用法

He, *who* had suffered..., was qualified to know

(Hailey *Hotel* 295)

(11) whose の代わりに用いる that's, its (Sc, AE, North Ir の informal な用法)。

This is the house *that's* roof fell in.

This is the house that *its* roof fell in.

第 4 章　冠詞

4.1　冠詞の交替

（1）the と a の交替

the majority / a majority

for a last time　　　　　　　　　　　(Steel *Paris* 102)

Peter had raised his voice to him, which was *a* first for him.

　　　　　　　　　　　　　　　　　　(Steel *Paris* 184)

（2）アクセントを欠く <h> で始まる語と an

a (an) historical book（1930 年代ですでに AE では確立）/ a (an) hotel / a (an) habitual visit (cf. a habit)

ただし a〜an herb (< F herbe [εrb])

（3）動詞・副詞結合（V-Adv）の名詞化と冠詞

{the / a} blowing up of a bridge / a coming together of two sounds / {the / a} coming together of British society / a chasing away of the ugly shadows / the closing down of thousands of factories

it seems to me such a hopeless filling in of desperate time

　　　　　　　　　　　　　　　　　(Drabble *Waterfall* 129)

4.2 the と both

N を修飾するときは both the boys。「両方」の意味のときも無冠詞が原則だが下例のように the を伴うことがある。

I'm sure she's more interesting than *the both* of us put together.

(Sheldon *Other* 193)

That must have been a very good thing for *the both* of you.

(Robbins *Goodbye* 47)

4.3 副詞の最上級と the

the を伴わない表現が標準と考えられていたが最近は伴うことも多い。

I enjoyed it *most* / fascinate her *the most*

the thing that disturbed Judd *the most* was　　(Sheldon *Naked* 144)

　　cf.　I'll call him *first thing* [= firstly] tomorrow.

第5章　形容詞

5.1　形容詞と節

① Adj が節を従える構文は古い時代からあり、PE になってその数を増していった。（ⅰ）Adj―{of / about} it that のような構文が想定される Adj、あるいは to 不定詞をとりうる Adj、（ⅱ）節を取る V や N と意味的、形態的に関連づけられる Adj。

（ⅰ）　afraid / angry / anxious / aware / careful / clear / confident / conscious / certain / glad / grateful / happy / lucky / nervous / right / sorry / sure / wrong

（ⅱ）　hope ― hopeful / desire ― desirable / believe ― incredible / remark ― remarkable / shame ― shameful / fear ― fearful / will―willing / insist―insistent / doubt―doubtful / confide―confident

② 関心、感情などを表す過去分詞

agreed / concerned / convinced / disappointed / delighted / determined / encouraged (I was encouraged that the audience was so big.) / finished / flattered / honored / pleased / puzzled / surprised / thrilled / terrified / touched / upset / undecided

(she was) *hurt* that her mother had cared so little for her
③ They were both very *proud* of themselves that they had gotten through the night without misbehaving. (Steel *Paris* 147)

5.2 形容詞化

① 名詞の形容詞化
限定用法が圧倒的。すっかり形容詞化されると叙述的となる。
Adj とならんでいる： She was lively, *fun*, intelligent
(Archer *First* 210)
a *champion* screamer / the highest *quality* wines / a *surprise* victory / a *wonder* boy / a *wonder* dog / a *fun* time / He was so much *fun* to be with / How *fun* is it? / very *fun* / the *fun* stuff / a heavy *gold* watch chain / *average* life

He was pretty *average*. (Dunning)
Honey was *average* (Sheldon *Nothing* 103)
It's fairly *standard* (Grisham *Runaway* 167)
She's *fun* to be with (Sanders *Pleasure* 156)
Lots of bright *fun* people (Robbins *Lady* 362)
Every single piece of equipment was *state of the art*
(Sheldon *Windmills* 19)
nothing *fancy* (Cornwell *All* 68)
it was very *fancy* for her (Steel *Ghost* 387)
give you *advance* warning (Cornwell *All* 175)

② 過去分詞の形容詞化
very などで修飾されたり、N を修飾する。
be very *pleased* / a *surprised* look

she remembered how *lost* she had been then

(Sheldon *Memories* 371)

5.3 a-形容詞の限定用法

まれながらみられる。

the most *alive* man she had ever met (Sheldon *Other* 192)
his attitude (was) one of *aloof* neutrality (Sheldon *Other* 448)
We're in an *aloof* mood, are we? (Sanders *Pleasures* 324)
a very *aware* lady (Robbins *Betsy* 43; Koontz *Moon* 202)
the slightly pale, *unafraid* kind (Koontz)

5.4 比較

(1) 絶対比較(最上)級 (absolute comparative (superative))
最近は、コマーシャルの影響で増えている。
women's *better* dresses / it makes you *prettier* / *best* for health
(2) 混交 (contamination) (ラジオ放送などで)
as expensive than / more expensive as
(3) curious + er
Curiouser and curiouser (Archer *Prod* 258)
   cf. *Alice's Adventures in Wonderland* (1865)
(4) lesser...than
lesser men *than* you are offered the channel to shape future policy
(Archer *First* 314)
(5) not as...as
今日では受け入れられている(1969年の数字によると賛成43%)。

第 6 章　副詞

6.1　否定

（1）否定辞と準動詞（verbals）

　① *not* to do と to *not*（*never*）do
　　後者は 20 世紀後半からみられる。
　　I'd rather *not* be there alone.
　　I suggest that it *not* be left alone.
　　to *never* give one thought to it again
　② *not* having done it と having *not* done it

（2）never

　　not と同じ働きの never（negative minimizer）が使われることがある（AE, BE ともに増えている）。

　　　　　　　　　　　　話しことば　書きことば

　　BE : I *never* stole that car.　40〜50%　　10%
　　I *never* broke it ［= I didn't break it］.
　　You will *never* catch the train.
　　I *never* read his press releases.　　　　（Archer *4th* 437）
　　I *never* did like the man.　　　　　　（Archer *Accidents* 176）

cf. only insane people were *never ever* scared

(Koontz *Moon* 429)

（3） 否定文のあとの No / Yes
 ① 先行文の内容の是認として（No）
 ② 先行文の内容に抗議、反対を表す（No）

"You do*n't* know anything" — "Oh, *no*!"
— Mary protested and went on, "I know a lot."
Shall I show her in? Ah, you're *not* receiving—Oh, *no*, *no*, show her in please.
Do*n't* you agree? — "*No*," she said. "I agree completely"

(Block *Hit* 184)

You do*n't* like Hugh much anything, do you? *No*.（「いいえ、好きだ」） I mean *yes*. *Yes*, I do quite like Hugh. (Drabble *Year* 72)
Would you mind reading for me? — *No*, certainly not.
I thought I ought to have a word with you in private, as I am sure you would *not* want us to prefer charges — *Yes*, *no*, of course, thank you for your consideration. (Archer *First* 357)

 ③ 日本人が否定の内容に反対するとき Yes というべきを No ということがあるが、native speaker もまちがえることがある。mind の場合は Yes / No いずれも 'go ahead' の意味なので許されている。

（4） 否定の scope
 ① intentionally / accidentally などは文中の位置によって否定の scope の内側、外側にあるかが決まる。

   [I *intentionally* did*n't* touch it].
   [I did*n't* touch it] *intentionally*.

 ② 助動詞と否定
   （ⅰ） 1) must / ought は「すべき」の意味で、may は「かもしれない」

(epistemic) の意味のとき否定の scope の外。
You must*n't* do it (= You're required [not to do it]). / It may [not be raining].

2) may は「してもよい」(deontic) のとき否定の scope の内。
You may *not* have any more (= [You are not permitted]...).

(ⅱ) If I don't *be* what I am, then I'm not being anything
(Drabble *Year* 62)

③ 数量詞と否定

(ⅰ) all, both の否定

scope の内側のとき部分否定 (partial negative)

I didn't solve *all* of the problems. / I didn't solve *both* the problems.

scope の外側のとき全否定 (total negative) (= none, neither)

Both of them don't think so [= None of them think so].

All of them don't think so [= Neither of them think so].

(ⅱ) some の否定

scope の外側のとき

Some people don't think so.

④ その他

always　　scope の内側のとき

　　　　　He doesn't *always* come home late.

very　　　主要部が否定の scope の内側のときは入る

　　　　　He did not behave *very* rudely.

because　 pause があるときは否定の scope の外側

　　　　　　　ないときは内側

I did *not* see a doctor, *because* I was afraid.

I did *not* see a doctor *because* I was sick.

Don't despise a man *because* he is poorly dressed.

(5) 英語では「年、背、深さ、高さ」など一般的なことをきくとき、否定の意味は有標(marked)なので用いない。

 how old...? *how young...?
 how tall...? *how short...?
 how deep...? *how shallow...?
 how high...? *how low...?

(6) 否定と also ～ too / already

also は否定とひんぱんに使われ、文頭におかれる。*too* は否定とそれほど使われないが許される。*already* が not と使われるときは疑問文同様、「おどろき」を表したり、Yes を期待するとき。しかし最近は *yet* と同じように使われる。

Also I can't tolerate the idea...

He *too* spoke no English.

I don't realize that you are a lawyer *too*. (Hailey *Airport* 359)

He wondered why they had not done so *already*.

            (Sheldon *Stars* 141)

He wouldn't let anything be discussed that they aren't *already* aware of. (Sheldon *Windmills* 260)

He quickly topped up her wine, pretending it hadn't *already* been poured. (Archer *Matter* 72)

Tell me something I don't *already* [= yet] know. (Dunning)

Sundy Kirk had *not already* collected the body. (Koontz *Fear* 31)

(7) not...as ～ as

not...as ～ as は not...so ～ as と同じくらい自然に受け入れられている。

(8) at all

否定、条件の文脈で用いられるが、それらの意味が内包されていると

きも、肯定文のようにみえるが、そうではないのでat all が用いられる。any があると用いられやすいのはそのためである。

You're nice to put up with me *at all.* / to the extent that she is *at all* like her mother / the problem of the need for *any* kind of food *at all* / He still wants to speak, to say anything *at all*.

（9）多重否定 don't（didn't）not…

I didn't say that. You didn't *not* say it *either*.

(Hailey *Wheels* 405)

Well, I don't believe and I don't *not* believe.

(Sanders *Pleasures* 22)

6.2 平坦副詞(flat adverb)

とくにAEの口語の特徴で、かつては俗語として-ly 形がすすめられたが今日では盛んに用いられる。今日ではBEでも用いられる。

go *slow*	（AEではすでに1940ごろまでに確立）			
	（1975年の数字：Yes	82%	No	18%）
feel real *bad*	（1975年の数字：Yes	77%	No	23%）
badly	（1975年の数字：Yes	26%	No	74%）
important（文副詞）	（1975：AE	Yes 75%	No	25%）
importantly（〃）	（1975：AE	Yes 25%	No	75%）

More *important*, it will work.

hold *tight* / go *quick* (*bad, proper*) / we were all *pretty* upset / sit *pretty* / work *pretty* good / *first* (*second, third*)

It *sure* is good. / I've *sure* heard a lot about you.（元来AEで第1文のような位置にあった。1940年ごろはまだ問題ありとされたが今日の口語ではふつう。）

(the short stop is playing) *deep*（深く守る）/ I'm dressed all

wrong. / do *fine* / I've to act *natural.* / fly *blind*

6.3 強調詞(intensifier)

(1) very / much
口語では very が盛んで、過去分詞(の Adj)にも拡大されてきている。by を伴う構文でも使われることがある。
  ① very / much で揺れるもの
    different / alive / afraid / hearted / astonished / surprised
  ② very が用いられるもの
    celebrated / polished / praised / delighted / amazed / pleased / irritated / disappointed / upset / amused / excited / tired / drunk / limited / damaged / determined
    He is *very* disturbed by your attitude.
    I'm *very, very* flattered by his offer.   (Sheldon *Windmills* 90)
  ③ (very) much がふつうの過去分詞
    criticized / disgusted / applauded / mistaken
  ④ thank you very much (a lot / a million) の代わりに thank you much が AE で 1960 年後半から聞かれ始め、1978 年以後拡大する。
(2) pretty / a lot
    a *pretty* good student / we were all *pretty* upset / it's *pretty* damaging / this is *a lot* more fun / it's *a lot* healthier than that
    Not *a lot* [= much]   (Archer *Matter* 89)
    He was *pretty* confused   (Grisham)
(3) 俗語では damn(ed) / the fuck / ass / bleeding (BE) などを用いて強める。
    she's *bleeding* well easy to forget
    damned good / *damn* young   (Steel *Passion* 40)

She was so *goddamn* tired of fighting with Bernardo.

(Steel *Love* 61)

It had been the *goddamnedest* thing he had ever seen

(Sheldon *Doomsday* 263)

（4） fucking / hell

It's four o'*fucking* clock in the morning! Who the＿?

(Sheldon *Windmills* 57)

I'm going to *fucking* put you away　　(Crichton *Disclosure* 241)

"Hell yes."　　　　　　　　　　　　　　　(Dunning)

（5） right

I'm *right* surprised.　　　　　　　(Cornwell *Body* 14)

（6） plenty

He was *plenty* stupid.　　　　　　(Grisham *Client* 487)

it's going to cost her *plenty*　　　(Sheldon *Sands* 262)

6.4　文副詞の発達

元来は「...のように」の意味の様態副詞でそれが文副詞へ発達した。hopefully［= it is hoped］

元来 AE で、1975 年では話しことばで賛成 42％、反対 58％、書きことばで賛成 24％、反対 76％。

BE では 1970 年代まで様態副詞だったが 1980 年代から入ってきた。

allegedly（19 c 末〜）/ reportedly（20 c 初め〜）/ justifiably / arguably（19 c 末〜）（しばしば比較級または最上級がつづく）/ understandably / acceptably（The first use is, *acceptably*, followed by the infinitive.）/ thankfully（*Thankfully*, it began to rain.）/ regrettably / honestly［= in fact］(I *honestly* don't know.) / supposedly / presumably / frankly［= to speak frankly］/ agreeably / unhappily

6.5 so

(1) say / do / believe / think / suppose / hope / be afraid / become などと共起する。また tell や know とはまれだが起こる。
Let me tell (John) *so*.
I know *so*　　　　　　　　　　　　(Robbins *Merchants* 506)

(2) hear / understand などは so I heard / so I understand という。tell も so he told のほうがふつう。

(3) look のような動詞とはふつう起こらないが、容認する人もいる。doubt / find out / prove なども so と起こらず it と起こる。
They say you're tough. You don't *look it*　　(Sheldon *Rage* 192)

cf. so = definitely
You *so* wouldn't. / I'm *so* in the front row. / I am *so* not happy.

6.6 副詞化

6.6.1 接続詞の副詞化

(1) though
元来接続詞だったものが 'however' の意味の副詞に転換されることがある。model は意味の似ている 'however'。また疑問文のあとでは強めの副詞として用いる。AE では 1970 年代でも 6 割以上が賛成。
Though he said he would come, he didn't. > He said he would come ; he didn't, *though*. / 'What a funny story !' said John. 'Isn't it, *though* ?'

(2) just in case
元来は節を導く接続詞であったが副詞として「万一に備えて」の意味を表す。

You'd better take an umbrella just *in case* (it rains).

handing over a thick manuscript. '*Just in case* you had nothing else to do.'　　　　　　　　　　　　　　　　　　(Archer *4th* 357)

(3) granted

最近、副詞として用いられる。

granted that... > granted

He's handsome—*granted* [= to be sure, of course, needless to say]

Granted, some of the fear I have for these parasites might be learned from my mother.

6.6.2 その他の副詞化

(1) 前置詞の副詞化

How did it work ?—Very well, *considering*. (割とうまくいった)
　　　　　　　　　　　　　　　　　　(Archer *Matter* 17)

(2) 形容詞＋前置詞の副詞化

it's *far from* [= *a long way from*] perfect　　(Block *Closet* 247)

the way she looked at him...was only a little *short of* conspicuous
　　　　　　　　　　　　　　　　　　(Robbins *Stallion* 267)

(3) that = so, this = so は最近の口語の発達である。

She's not *that* light a sleeper.　　　　　　　(Simon)

With *that* powerful a motive　　(Archer *Thieves* 120)

this tense a search for him　　(Sheldon *Doomsday* 363)

It's *this* simple / *this* often.

that many transatlantic calls (BE)

I'm not *that* surprised. (BE)

He's not *that* big a fool　　(Sheldon *Memories* 377)

that 〜 that... (= so 〜 that...)

I don't look *that* much older than you *that* we can't be mistaken for sisters. (Robbins *Stiletto* 171)

I'm not *that* old that I don't know what's on your mind.

(4) place / time を第2要素とする名詞を副詞として
some place (AE) / any place / every place / no place (AE) / some (any) time / every time (AE では1950年ごろ確立)

(5) home
at などの前置詞を落して副詞化する。1940年ごろにはAEでは確立している。
John was *home* all last week.

(6) approaching 'nearly' (1960年ごろから)
approaching half the Lancashire cotton industry

6.7 注意すべきその他の副詞

(1) answer in the affirmative (negative) は口語では answer yes (no) という。

(2) 「どれ位前から」は
How *long since* you've gotten a raise? という。

(3) could care less が couldn't care less 「少しも気にしない」の意味で1960年ごろからAEで使われ始める。

(4) 肯定文の anymore
'now' の意味で元来アメリカの West Virginia などの方言だったが1945年ごろから口語に入り始める。しかし否定文と使うべきとする意見が強く反対する人も多い。
I want you to see me by appointment *anymore*.

(5) sufficiently 〜 that... と 〜 enough that... [= so 〜 that...]
the population in the country is *sufficiently* small that 〜
It was cool *enough* out that I could see his breath

(Cornwell *Unnatural* 121)

(6)　there

　　There had better not be any more accidents （Higgins *Season* 43）

(7)　well

　　well＋過去分詞が標準だったが最近若い人たちの間では well＋形容詞（*well* angry）が聞かれつつある。

(8)　like

　　最近 approximator（いわゆる「ぼかし表現」）として 'just, something like' の意味で使われることがある。

　　They are *like* three (3 years old).

　　like a loan furniture company

(9)　alongside

　　'together with, as well as' の意味での用法が新聞などの financial pages でみられる。

(10)　momentarily「一瞬」の意味だけでなく「直ちに」の意味でも用いる（20 c から）。

(11)　presently「やがて」の意味だけでなく「現在」の意味でも用いる（元来 AE。しかし 1975 年現在で賛成 16％－反対 84％。BE へも入る）。

(12)　one day「（過去の）ある日」の意味だけでなく「（未来の）ある日」の意味でも用いる。

(13)　even を 'just' の意味で用いる even as

　　even as she turned, she knew who it was （Sheldon *Stranger* 277）

　　even as Robert thought it, he heard the sound of a helicopter

　　　　　　　　　　　　　　　　　　　　　　（Sheldon *Doomsday* 426）

　　even as he was thinking it, the doorbell rang

　　　　　　　　　　　　　　　　　　　　　　（Sheldon *Nothing* 332）

　　The little white stick kept moving toward the red patch *even as* Adam watched it　　　　　　　　　　（Archer *Matter* 235）

(14) too

　　　句の頭位で 'in addition, moreover' の意味で用いる (AE)。

　　　He got like that. But, *too*, he was a charmer.

(15) be busily -ing 〜 be busy -ing

　　　元来は be busy -ing 構文であったものがおそらく、

　　　He was at the desk, busily writing... > He was busily writing...

　　　というようになったか、be busy -ing の類推で生じたものと思われる。しばしばみられる。

(16) sort of / kind of (この種の「ぼかし表現」に用いることばを hedge と呼ぶ。)

　① 元来 AE。BE でも用いられた。

　　　1 語の degree modifier で 16 c 末にはじめて起こる。

　　　1800 年以前は [kind]$_N$ とも [kind of]$_{Adv}$ とも解していた。

　　　19 c になると Adv の解釈が確立する。

　　　1940 年ごろの AE では問題ありとされたがその後確立する。

　② 構造の特色

　　　(i) (a) kind of a cat の (a) はとらず

　　　(ii) ＿A (*kind of* hungry)

　　　　　＿VP (*kind of* cried out)　　　　のような文脈で用いられる。

　　　　　Det＿AN (a *kind of* big rock)

　　　　　V＿N (is *kind of* an island)

(17) noway [= never]

　　　Noway mail service is going to improve.

　　　Noway will you stop prices or unemployment going up again.

第7章 前置詞

7.1 前置詞の交替

前置詞の交替は元来、意味上の重複があり、生起する構造が同じであるので、容易に起こる。

(1) to / than / about〜over

agree to > agree *over* / like A better than B > like A *over* B / prefer A to B > prefer A *over* B / quarrel about > quarrel *over*

(2) to〜than

prefer to walk *than* to cycle

It's superior *than* attempting.

(3) wait for〜on

They waited *on* Jake　　　　　　　(Grisham *Time* 450)

(4) look at〜to

He looked *to* the front row in the courtroom

(Grisham *Time* 157)

(5) different from〜than (BE, AE)〜to (BE)

than は AE では一般にほぼ受入れられているが BE でも今日ではまれではなくなっている。to はとくに BE の口語で特にひんぱんにみ

られる。書きことばにも起こる。

Whatever happens here is different *to* what is allowed to happen elsewhere.

(6) of〜about

about が盛んとなる。

inform one of〜about ／ remind one of〜about ／ be aware about ／ be disdainful about

(7) of〜from

It's ten minutes' walk of〜from the station ／ independent of〜from
It was within three days *from* July 7　　　(Forsyth *Jackal* 52)
Time hadn't robbed it *from* him　　　(Robbins *Storyteller* 339)

(8) in〜with〜of

abound in〜with〜of

pictures abound *of* family, children and grandchildren

(Simon *Red* 585)

(9) on〜in

on〜in the morning of Sunday

　cf. in the morning ／ on Sunday morning

on behalf of (BE) だが、AE では on behalf of の他に in behalf of も用いられる。

(10) at〜on

① knock at〜on the door
② on〜at the weekend

at は BE、on は AE で好まれる。

cf.　over the weekend

(11) with〜from

be tired with〜from

(12) of〜for

in search of～for

この for は動詞の search *for*, make a search *for* からの影響で AE にみられる慣用だがまだ確立していない。

accuse me of～for flinching from him　　　　　　　(Drabble)

(13)　with～to

talk with～to May

(14)　on～of

I'll think *on* it　　　　　　　(Robbins *Pred* 284)

(15)　with～about

disagree with～about what you've said

(16)　at～with～of

He was getting nervous again, terrified *of* making a mistake

(Sheldon *Doomsday* 158)

(17)　suffer from～over it　　　　　　　(Grisham)
(18)　stick to～with the facts
(19)　to the contrary (AE)　～*on* the contrary (BE)
(20)　glad of～at the words　　　　　　　(Klavan *Crime* 330)

7.2　前置詞の残留 (p-stranding)

7.2.1　PPからの取り出し

　前置詞句(PP)からの取り出しは原則的にはNの補部(complement)のとき(i.e. N領域内)のみ可能。
しかし付加詞(adjunct)のPPから取り出される場合もある。

Who(m) did you take a picture of?   *Which city did you meet a man from?

I've got a problem I'm hoping you can help me *with*

(Cornwell *All* 266)

put the tags back on the car I'd stolen them *from*

(Cornwell *All* 313)

it is a hammer that he broke the vase *with*

a book that he spends much money *on*

You don't smoke cigars. —to pose *with*　　(Block *Kipling* 219)

　　cf. money was something he had a ton *of*　　　(Block *Hit* 176)

7.2.2　2重前置詞構造

　P—which—X—P といった2重前置詞構文がみられることがある。
　Pが同じでくり返される場合((a))、2つのPが異なる場合((b))がみられる。
　この構文はMEではふつうでP—which—X—Adv(AdvはPから出た関連形が用いられた：in—inne / on—onne)
　この構文は余剰的(誤り)ともみられるが、英語ではXが長い要素で、その一部が右へ動かせる(extrapose)こと((c))や、動かさないで宙づり(stranded)のままにしておける((d))ことと関係があろう。

（a）the work *in* which you are interested *in*

　　　many fields *from* which to choose *from*

　　　rates *for* which he is paying *for*

（b）the direction *in* which he came *from*

　　　my memories, *in* which I came back *to*

　　　four years of studies *of* which he can't earn a living *by*

（c）jobs *in* which they'd like to do literature *in* which they studied

（d）the one Tyler wanted to spend the rest of his life *with*

7.3　前置詞化

（1）　接続詞の前置詞化

as far as は前置詞化して NP をとることができる。ただし、代名詞は不可。これは as far as NP *is concerned* / *goes* の省略とみることができ、'as for, with regard to' の意味を表す。いまのところ AE の慣用(cf. Richford, et al. (1995))だが、American Heritage Dictionary によると動詞のない形は 165 人中 84% が反対している。

as far as the white servant, it is clear

*as far as me / I

as far as actually planning a crime, I don't think so

(Grisham *Time* 53)

As far as *how I got him*, it happened pretty much the way I said

(Block *Williams* 100)

as far as *making up the building's annual deficit*

（2）　分数・倍数

it was only a monkey and hardly *a fourth* my weight(〜の 4 分の 1)

(Koontz *Fear* 115)

most surfers *a third* his age　　　　　(Koontz *Fear* 190)

a woman *twice* her age

（3）　形容詞(句)の前置詞化

short of を 'without' の意味で用いる。

There was no way to shut him up *short of* killing him.

(Koonts *Fear* 285)

7.4　問題のある前置詞

（1）　before と in front of

最近の英語では before は時間に用い空間には使わなくなってきている。

There is a big tree {*before / in front of} the house.

（2）　behind と in back of と back of

in back of は AE で今日口語でよく使われるようになってきている。ここから派生した back of については反対意見が多い。

There is a big tree {behind / in back of / back of} my house

（3）　to〜till / until

場所に till / until も用いることがある。

It will be my secret *till* the grave.　　(Sheldon *Windmill* 197)

　　cf. a secret I'll carry *to* the grave　　　　　　(ibid.)

The occupants of the van...must be employed by the unknown people who manipulated him so ruthlessly *until* Kansas City

(Koontz *Murder* 375)

（4）　due to

元来 AE 起源で 1960 年代に BE にも入ってきたがそのころは問題のある表現とされた。しかし最近は確立した表現として受入れられている。

Due to his nervousness she made a slip.

（5） between〜among

1960 年代までは「2 か 3 以上」により使いわけることが強く主張されていたが、最近でも一部の人たちはそう主張する。しかし、しばしば each other と one another の区別と同様無差別に使われる。

第 8 章　接続詞

（1）　if［＝ whether］

19 c から最初 be 動詞の後位置で。その後他の文脈に拡大される。ただし to do は as if のあとは許されるが if to do は不可。

The question is if it is right (or not).

I don't know if it is right.（1940 年ごろ AE ですでに確立）

If it is right or not is... ／ I'm not sure if...

he's not sure if she is a gift to him or he to her

(Koontz *Intensity* 224)

ただし、まだ P や the question のあとは不可。

depend on whether or not S ／ *depend on if or not S

the question whether〜 ／ *the question if〜

He had no idea if that was what the precocious pooch wanted him to do.　(Koontz *Watchers* 64)

He had *no idea* if he was being invited to tea　(Steel *Ghost* 68)

Sarah had *no idea* if François had survived it.

(Steel *Ghost* 381-2)

I wonder *whether* ／ *if to go

（2）　the reason is because...

AE ですでに 1940 年ごろ確立。BE でも受け入れられている。

 cf. the reason *why* it is late coming out is {that / because}...

 cf. Tell me *the way how you did it

(3) like

とくに feel / look / seem / sound / be などのあとで用いられる。とくに AE の口語体で使われるが、いまなお反対意見も強い。BE でも少しずつ認められている。

Do it *like* I tell you.

It was *like* a fantasy come true. (Sheldon *Nothing* 309)

It's not *like* he was out there in the woods alone

          (Cornwell *All* 132)

It's *like* [＝as] if someone dies (Steel *Ghost* 19)

We can make it look *like* he contributed important things to the stallion [＝car] (Robbins *Stallion* 129)

(4) on account of

on account of I saw it [＝slay] here yesterday

        (Block *Williams* 159 ; 284)

(5) for as long as

for as long as I have to (Steel *Paris* 253)

(6) as... as (譲歩)

She didn't doubt Marty's story, *as* wild *as* it was [＝ wild though it was]. (Koontz *Murder* 185)

(7) no matter that〜

All these types of words are valid parts of the English language, *no matter that* they are old and obsolete or new...

        (Winchester *Prof* 105)

(8) except[＝ unless]

Okay. *Except* Mr Lowbertein hates me (Klavan *Crime* 161)

第9章　動詞

9.1　時制

(1) 完了

① 現在完了と過去形

口語では現在完了 (最近終了したことを示す) の代りに過去形が一般的になりつつある。最初は AE で、最近は BE のとくに若い人の間でよく聞かれる (Hughes & Trudgill (1979:9))。just, ever のような副詞で過去とのつながりを示す (news 性を与えるためとする説がある)。

What happened to your face?

I *just* moved (to a new house).

a new French restaurant that *just* opened

I *just* remembered

Did you *ever* hear the news?

I *never* saw you before in my life　　　　　(Simon *Little* 90)

Have you seen a male secretary before?

—No. *Didn't* know men could be secretaries

(Grisham *Client* 204)

He gets his money and goes back the same way he *came* [= he has come］(来たとおりに帰る)　　　　　　　(Cornwell *Potter's* 336)

② 短い時の過去の副詞と現在完了が共起することがある。最近の英語に現れ始めた。なお、ScE、IrE などにもみられる。AE だけでなく BE でもみられる。

I've seen her *last year* / *last week*.

He's done it *two days ago*.

これらは afterthought 的な用法と考えられ、したがって *Last year I've seen her. は不可。

③ be＋過去分詞の完了

go / come がほとんど唯一の動詞である。ただし3人称単数主語と共起する 's は have とも be ともとれる。finish は形容詞とも自動詞の完了形ともとれる。gather は文脈からみて他動詞ではないので完了の可能性がある。変移動詞(mutative verb)の be＋過去分詞の完了形は go を除き 1900 年ごろ消えた。

Peter *was gone* [= disappeared].

at last our dream *is come* true　　　　　(Simon *Little* 135)

How soon will you *be finished* (with it)?

I'*m* nearly *finished*. I *have* nearly *finished*. They *were finished* talking.

As soon as you'*re finished* testifying　　　(Sheldon *Rage* 479)

there are many reasons why we *are gathered* here today

(Sheldon *Rage* 383)

we *are* all *gathered* here on this joyous occasion (Simon *Little* 74)

④ narrative tense

語りの伝達動詞は he said, he says(「史的現在」)がふつうだが最近 he says…he has said…he says のような完了形をとる伝達動詞がみられるようになった。読者の注意を引く効果を狙ったものかもしれない。

（2） be like 構文
① ダイアローグ導入語句 (dialogue introducer) として最近 AE (この 20～30 年の間) で用いられるようになった。起源はよくわからないが (cf. Romaine & Lange (1991)) つぎの特徴をもつ。
（ⅰ） 1) 'say, go' の意味で直接引用文を導入する。
2) 'think, say to oneself' の意味を表す。
ある数字によれば be like 8%に対し say 43%、go 13%
（ⅱ） 現在、過去いずれにも用いられる。また人称に対する制限もない。
I am (was) like / you are (were) like / she is (was) like
（ⅲ） 性、地域といった社会的要因は働かないが、とくに若い人の口語、語りの文体で用いられる。間接話法や疑問文には拡がっていない。
I'm like, "This is my senior year."
And she was like, "No."
　　cf. He goes, "I was tired."
　　　　*He goes that he was tired.

②

(ⅰ)	時制	現在	過去	
	say	24%	67%	
	go	61%	3%	
	be like	71%	28%	
(ⅱ)	年令	20-24才	27-32才	38-72才
	say	35.9%	48.9%	65%
	go	79.9%	24.3%	43.9%
	be like	68.1%	31.9%	—
(ⅲ)		平叙文	疑問文	感嘆文
	say	69%	64%	19%

		1人称	3人称単数	3人称複数
	go	16%	29%	92%
	be like	—	—	—
(iv)		1人称	3人称単数	3人称複数
	say	42%	66%	47%
	go	45%	70%	44%
	be like	43%	26%	45%

（ⅴ）男性(53%)－女性(47%)(Blyth, Recktenwald and Wang (1990))

③ like to ＞ liketa [＝ almost] died(文法化の1つ)

　　cf. You (su) poseta went there [＝ You are supposed to have gone there].

　　cf. Brandy ?-Like to.

　　cf. wanna / usedto / haveta / hasta / a coupla Japs

9.2 進行形

（1）進行形をとらない動詞のリスト(perception verbs, emotion verbs, wishing verbs)

① dislike / hate / like / love / prefer / want / wish / astonish / impress / please / satisfy / surprise

② believe / doubt / feel / guess / imagine / know / mean / realize / recognize / remember / suppose / think / understand

③ hear / see / measure / taste / smell / sound / weigh

④ belong to / concern / consist of / resemble / contain / depend on / deserve / fit / include / involve / lack / matter / need / owe / own / possess / have

⑤ appear / seem

　　he's probably *remaining* out of sight　　　　(Hailey *Hotel* 358)

（2）実際は（1）であげた動詞のほとんどが進行形をとる。とくに「一時的

な行為」「くり返しの行為」を表すとき。しかし、これらの意味を表すときでなくても進行形が起こる事実から、PE では大多数の動詞の型を無標として進行構文が侵食しつつあるのであろう。(1)の動詞は右から左へ進みつつある。

  進行形がふつう　　　　　進行形にならない

  ⟵─────────────

   do love   seem
   go like   appear
           matter

AE: Oklahoma ではほとんどの動詞が進行形となる。
be wanting to / I'*m understanding* / *are* you *knowing* / *Is* your food *tasting* all right?

(3) I would *be loving* you if I could manage it. (Drabble *Year* 131)
certainly he'*s liking* me
This is what I have *been wanting* for many years.
I've *been wanting* to meet you.
        (Archer *4th* 220; Sheldon *Stars* 224)
the question that he...had *been wanting* to ask for weeks
           (Koontz *Moon* 263)
Perce had *been understanding*, realizing that S (Hailey *Wheels* 402)
She *was remembering* how
The butcher *was weighing* the meat.
He *was seeing* her for a while.
She could not believe what she *was hearing*.
One of my boys *is having* a problem.
He *was having* a quick whisky.
be having a good day / an affair / a financial problem
I'*m having* your baby.   (Sheldon *Nothing* 302)

Is my ex-wife *having* me followed?

 cf. he *was* now *knowing* and astute (Sanders *Pleasures* 188)
the director, who had *been hoping* to...
It's *looking* [= seem] a pretty good bet for me (Archer *4th* 265)
how much *are* those two *costing* me? (Archer *4th* 471)
the demons *were seeming* to have a depressing influence

          (Winchester *Prof* 124)

the name *was seeming* more appropriate with every passing hour

            (Block *Hit* 48)

9.3 受身

（1）進行形に比べると受身に抵抗する動詞の数は多い。それは、文体や、受身が起こることが許される環境の制限と、受身に代わる代替表現（例えば have 構文、能動文）が得られるためと思われる。
constitute / weigh / resemble / become / have / contain / bet (10 dollars) / last / grow (onions) / lack / hold / fit / suit / cost
（2）受身の助動詞の代表は be だがその他に become, stand などがあるが口語では get が圧倒的である。
（3）2つの目的語をとる構文の受身
 ① 史的には間接目的語は、副詞的な意味で使われていたので(for〜, to〜)、受身の主語になれなかった(cf.ドイツ語)が、時代とともに受身の主語として使われるように拡がってきた。しかし、今日でもまだその制限は残る。1950 年代の BE では write, send, owe の間接目的語の受身は受入れられなかったが、今日では AE 同様許されている。
A long letter *was written* to her. / She *was written* a long letter.
A note *was sent* to him. / He *was sent* a note.

An injustice *was done* to him. / He *was done* an injustice.
The trouble *was spared* me. / I *was spared* the trouble.
The Germans *were served* coffee.
He *was allowed* no visitors.
the money that *was owed* them　　　(Sheldon *Bloodline* 246)
Cynthia would have many contacts; a city commissioner could bestow favors and *was owed* them in return

(Hailey *Detective* 569)

I'*m being sent* a picture by my fellow.　(Sheldon *Doomsday* 217)

② 利益／不利益の間接目的語の受身は今日なお抵抗がある。必ず2つの目的語を要求する cost one 10 dollars の受身は許されない。
that 節を伴うときは、間接目的語の主語または it による直接目的語の受身となる。

*We were read an interesting story.

*He was made a good wife by Mary.

*John was made a suit.

*I was bet a hundred dollars.

?I was fetched something to drink.

{ *Nothing was cost me.
{ *I was cost nothing

{ I was informed that he was killed in an accident.
{ It was informed me that～

(4) graduate, want、自動詞などの受身

① graduate

元来 AE では be graduated from がふつうであったが1950年以降 graduate from にとって代られていった。今日まだ受身がみられるが、AE、BE とも能動形が一般的である (Sheldon には時に be graduated from がみられる)。

② want
　　She would have to know what she *was wanted* to do
　　　　cf. He knew what *was wanted*　　　　(Robbins *Xanadu* 91)
③ その他
　　This house *was lived in* by three monarchs.
　　the bed...as if it had not *been slept in*
　　He felt he'd *been lied to* and cheated　　　(Cornwell *All* 175)
　　Most of a floor never *gets walked on*　　　(Sanders *Pleasures* 97)
　　The fork *is eaten with.* / The bed seems to have *been slept in*.
　　My mind *was made up*.　　　　　　　　(Cornwell *All* 319)
　　　　cf. make up one's mind〜make one's mind up
　　Their minds *are made up*.　　　　　　　(Grisham *Time* 347)
　　He didn't like *being disagreed with*　　　(Crichton *Disclosure* 321)
　　She didn't like to *be differed with*.　　　(Robbins *Stranger* 275)
　　I *was rained on* yesterday.（雨に降られた）

9.4　仮定法

PE の仮定法の生起は非常に局地化されている。とくに AE の影響で、一時化石化されていた仮定法が文語として一部復活しているようにみえる（とくに 1960 年代から）。ただし BE では助動詞を使う方がふつうである。
　　He suggested that I come tomorrow.
従節では直説法も使われる。
　　it's important that buses are banned from the city centre.
仮定法は、慣用表現として残っている表現が主節に起こるのを除くと、従節に集中して起こる。
　　Heaven *forbid* / God *save* the Queen
BE でも増えつつある。とくに formal style で demand, insist, suggest など

のあとの文や as if, if などの節で用いられる。

(1) 仮定法の生起場所

① if, on condition, as if, as though, lest, suppose, imagine につづく節中で(ただし suggest, would rather でも直説法現在が起こることもある)

if it *were* still true

on condition that she *play* the lead

as if he *were* dead

He was afraid, lest they *poison* his food.

lest their morals *be* contaminated

if it *was*n't for the high cost of the Swiss franc

(Archer *Matter* 119)

you'd rather I *do*n't this time　　　(Block *Hit* 117)

he says as if Kipler *has*...helped him immensely

(Grisham *Rainmaker* 312)

Van wondered if he *were* not being left in a barbaric land.

(Robbins *Stallion* 261)

　cf. suggests that Perino *uses* it on the condition that Carpenter *continue* to telephone Loren

② suggest / propose / ask / request / demand / insist / command / order / urge / recommend およびこれらの動詞から出た名詞(insistence / suggestion / proposal など)、または似た意味の名詞(句)(move / demand / in his demand)などにつづく従節中で用いる。that は1語の root 形の仮定法がつづく marker なので省略されにくい(⇒ 省略)。

He asked that she *leave*.

he was determined there *be* no trace of a Polish accent...

(Archer *Prod* 16)

③ I wish / I'd rather / I prefer / 'd as soon につづく節で用いる。

I wish it *were* over.

I wish you *had*n't done it.

wishing that he *were* more than just semiconscious

(Steel *Gift* 247)

I'd rather you *went* home now.

このいい方は AE で早く確立し、1940 年ごろから認められるようになった。

the XB accidents would rather I *spend* my time sitting around...

(Robbins *Stallion* 302)

He preferred that his client *try* to get a good night's sleep

(Archer *K&A* 536)

She preferred that the trial *be* held here (Sheldon)

I'd just as soon you *did*n't (Robbins *Stallion* 237)

④ it is necessary / essential / important / desirable / vital / impossible につづく節内で用いる。

it is logically *possible* that it *be* fixed (Culicover 1997:356)

it is *important* that he *talk* to Anne

it is *impossible* that he *come* and that he *stay*

⑤ it is time につづく節中で用いる。なおそれ以上つづく節では抵抗する。最初の節にのみ影響し、さらに埋めこまれた節には及ばない。ただし it is time の文脈に少しずつ直説法が入り込み始める。

It is time he *changed* this car for a new one.

It is time that this great body *realized* that it is its sworn duty to precious heritage (Sheldon *Doomsday* 259)

    cf. it's time you *take* on an independent inquiry

(Sanders *Trial* 139)

⑥ 不確定なことを表すとき

All that mattered was that she *escape*　　　(Sheldon *Other* 408)

（2） was / were の選択

口語では was が好まれる（1969 年の AE の統計でも 74%が was を受け入れる）。

I wish it *were*（*was*）true.

if it *were*（*was*）still at school, I would work

she felt as though she *were*（*was*）about to be sentenced to death

as if he *were*（*was*）crazy

it was time that I *was* sent to the secondary school

BE でも if I *were* you よりも if I *was* you の方が自然である。

If I *was* you, I would quit. は 1998 年（Michigan の学生）では informal ではよいが formal では半分ぐらいが不可としている。

（3） 倒置条件（inverted condition）

ふつうは Aux, be, have に起こるが、まれに come に起こる。

It's been rumored that *come* the next presidential election, P. Harvey may successfully conclude what G. Ferraro started

(Cornwell *All* 58)

　　cf. *come* what may, provided he remained alive, he was a wealthy man for the rest of his life

come the crisis [= if the crisis come], he would need Einstein's full powers　　　(Koontz *Watchers* 456)

9.5　自動詞〜他動詞

PE の特徴の 1 つに自動詞〜他動詞の混用がある。とくに能格動詞（ergative verb: break, open）、中間動詞（middle verb: cut, translate）などは広く行われている。

He smokes cigars〜He smokes ／ He drinks a beer〜He drinks ／ He expects a caller〜He expects ／ I meet Mary〜We meet

しかし、目的語を略さないものもある(use, abandon, finish)。自動詞が他動詞化したり、またその逆に他動詞が自動詞化する現象は現代英語の特徴で、これからますますその傾向を押しすすめていくと思われる。

歴史的にみると自動詞が他動詞化されていくのが主流であるが、現代英語の観点からみると1つの動詞がそのまま他動詞にも自動詞にも使うことができるということになる。

他動詞化のルートは
① 自動詞が前置詞をとり、さらに内容節をとるために it that となり、その it を削除、さらに full NP をとるようになる。その後、疑似分裂文(pseudo cleft: What ＿ is NP)が可能となり、さらに他動詞の最終段階として受身が可能となる。
② 自動詞＋前置詞の前置詞を落としたあと that 節をとるか、NP をとるようになる。
③ 自動詞が途中の段階を経ず内容節をとるか、NP をとるようになる。

VI → VI P → P it that 節 → that 節 → NP(→受身)

think のような動詞は think about〜 ／ think that 節(あるいは think wh-節：I cannot think what her name is)はあっても think NP はまれで(いずれ NP をうしろにとるかもしれない)まだ十分に他動詞化したとはいえない。

自動詞化のルートは
① 目的語が文脈から明らかな場合省かれることから始まり、直接自動詞の終着点へ到達するか、
② 前置詞を入れるようになる。

```
V NP→Vφ→VI
    ＼  ／
    V P NP
```

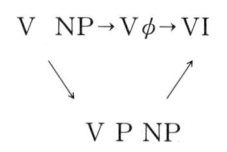

9.5.1 他動詞化

① it that をとる動詞

なお、自動詞でも it をつけて他動詞化できる (live it「ついていく」、go it「どんどんやる」、come it「うまくやる」)。

I *want* it (clear) that...

want that S (AE, BE とも。Burchfield(1996:832))

You *want* I should maybe knock on her door?　　　(Dunning)

You *want* maybe I should comment on this?　　　(Dunning)

I *love* it that he sits there

I *loved* that I could arouse him like that　　(Dickey *Friends* 131)

I *liked* it that the boy said 'please'.　　(Sheldon *Rage* 323)

I *like* that you never cut me any slack.　　(Koontz *Fear* 12)

He *hated* it that he had to spend every Christmas alone.

I *hate* that Ellen will miss it.　　(Grisham *Time* 460)

Our theory *has* it that the term originated in England.

this *has* as a natural consequence that only the syllables...in (2.3.2) can syncopate　　(Hammond 1997:50)

He can't *stand* [= endure] it that I got the job (as Ambassador)
　　　　　　　　　　　　　　(Sheldon *Windmills* 212)

Shall we just *leave* it that I won't hurry the process along until you tip me the mink?　　(Archer *4th* 193)

I can't *help* it that S(it はとれないが What I can't help is that〜は許される(Jespersen(1937:§22.2))。

② it を落したあと that 節をとるようになったもの
　(ⅰ)　agree that < agree on it / consent that < consent at it / comment that < comment on it / argue that < argue about it / boast that < boast of it / allow that < allow for it / repent that < repent at it / lament that < lament over it / marvel that < marvel at it / check that < check on it / beware that < beware of it / complain that < complain about it / insist that < insist on it / rejoice that < rejoice at it / hint that < hint at it / care that < care for it / think that < think about it / scream that < scream for it / brag that < brag of it / resolve that < resolve on it / arrange that < arrange about it

　　I like to *check* that... 　　　　　　(Hailey *Airport* 329)

　　He *despairs* that the Baron might send him back to the cottage
　　　　　　　　　　　　　　　　　　　(Archer *K&A* 33)

　　see (to it) that / cf. take care (of it) that / take note (of it) that / take hold (of it) that / bring (it) out that / bring (it) about that / cry out that / work out that / write down that

　　Everything about him *cried out* that he was needy
　　　　　　　　　　　　　　　　　　(Cornwell *All* 149)

　　I *picked up* that she might be in some sort of dangers
　　　　　　　　　　　　　　　　　　(Cornwell *All* 142)

　　We can't *rule out* that the murders of Deborah and her boyfriend were disguised to resemble the other cases(可能性を除けない)　　　　　　　　　　　(Cornwell *All* 182)

　(ⅱ)　make (it) sure that / make (it) certain that / have (it) in common that / keep (it) in mind that / take (it) for granted that

{参考} 形容詞にも同様の現象が起こる。

    be aware that < be aware of / be afraid that < be afraid of / be angry that < be angry at / be sure that < be sure of / be satisfied that < be satisfied with / be surprised that < be surprised at / be convinced that < be convinced of

    She was *scandalized*(憤慨した)that he had asked her.

                                                  (Robbins *Stallion* 213)

③ 前置詞を落としたあと NP をとるようになったもの

protest (against) some actions by the US(AE ではすでに 20 c 初めから。最近 BE でもみられる)

fail (in) the course(とくに AE で 1955 年以降みられる)

fight (against) the pain

No party can *fight* an election with its leader laid up in bed for six weeks   (Archer *First* 456)

walk the street in New York / Let me *walk* you to your room / She was *walked* down a long corridor.

sip (at) the coffee

crave (for)

Odd scraps of paper *lay*（現在形として）like puddles on the floor.

                                                  (Grisham *Rainmaker* 35)

graduated (from)（AE）

escape (from)(最近 NP をとるようになった)

seek (for) more information

agonize (over)

run (through) the world

    cf. he *worried* that he would have an anxiety attack

                                                  (Koonz *Survivor* 168)

    don't *worry* that you're letting down a friend

he...sat over coffee to *wait* it out (Archer *4th* 100)
 (Dunning)
you're *thinking* it / The police are *thinking* it. (Cornwell *All* 26)
As for caliber, I'm *thinking* a thirty-eight... (Cornwell *All* 97)
I can't tell you why I'm *thinking* this / that. (Cornwell *All* 139)
it was precisely what he'd been *thinking* (Steel *Ghost* 49)
When you hear the words *blue chip* what are you *thinking*?
I'll tell you what I'm *thinking*. I'm *thinking* Mickey Mantle. (〜のことを考える)

 cf. Keller wasn't sure what he *thought of* when he heard the words blue chip (Block *Hit* 126)
we...*talked* some more (Dunning)

④ 自動詞が途中の段階を経ずに that 節をとるか、または NP をとるようになったもの

（ⅰ） *dream* that some was trying to drown you
I *read* (in a newspaper) that you were hit by a car
 (Sheldon *Naked* 110)
He *joked* that it did not matter. (Archer *Other* 144)
estimate that S / *emphasize* that S (Robbins *Goodbye* 12)
nod that he understood (Sheldon *Naked* 46)
He *nodded* to the waiter that we were ready for coffee
 (Cornwell *All* 185)
She *whispered* over and over that she loved him...
 (Klavan *Crime* 234; Grisham *Time* 10)
(murmur / chortle / whine / lisp / whisper は that 節をとらないという人もある)
she *snarled* that her son hadn't gotten in...
 (Cornwell *Unnatural* 210)

His breathing *sang* that he wanted me （Dickey *Friends* 134）

I'm willing to *gamble* that he's changed. （Sanders *Secret* 227）

we can...*gamble* that Willigan will never learn we have told the police about it　　　　　　　　　　　　（Sanders *Luck* 131）

Swanson and Fitch were *gambling* that after Claire and Jeff left Lawrence they had not kept in touch with Beverly
　　　　　　　　　　　　　　　　　　（Grisham *Runaway* 414）

{参考}　that 節をとるまれな例

She never *planned* that you would get all the answers
　　　　　　　　　　　　　　　　　　（Robbins *Xanadu* 279）

he'll *respect* that you are a real man　（Robbins *Pred* 183）

I didn't *offer* that Abby had been with me　（Cornwell *All* 265）

You'd *deny* that a good innkeeper can stamp his personal imprint on any house？　　　　　　　　　　　（Hailey *Hotel* 173）

he...had long since *accepted* that he was tethered to her for life
　　　　　　　　　　　　　　　　　　（Archer *First* 25）

he *accepted* that his job was gone　（Hailey *Wheels* 236）

（Culicover (1976:258) は accept that... は非文としている）

Janette is my big sister. Sometimes we *play* that she's my mother. Just pretend.　　　　　　　　　　　（Robbins *Goodbye* 153）

I'm ready to *face* that she might turn out not to be Nina.
　　　　　　　　　　　　　　　　　　（Koontz *Survivor* 253）

...*intuited* that the monkeys were not the entire story
　　　　　　　　　　　　　　　　　　（Koontz *Fear* 234）

（ii）　the house *sleeps* five people

　　　the crew *sank* the ship ／ we're *flying* passengers

　　　disappear [＝ cause to disappear]

cf. The dissidents were *disappeared* in 1983. (最近の AE でみられる。)

sit a boy on the sofa

the other guard *sat* him in it　　　　　(Grisham *Chamber* 93)

he kindly *sat* me on a bench　　　　(Cornwell *Unnatural* 365)

stand the chair

I can't *stand* him. (すでに AE では 1940 年ごろ確立した)

he *stood* the tree on the ground next to her　(Steel *Gift* 232)

live a lie by cancelling her past

live a lie for the past three months (3ヶ月うその生活をする)

　　　　　　　　　　　　　　　　　(Block *Williams* 104)

You will also *cease* any further payments to Miss Janet Durrow immediately　　　　　　　　　　　(Archer *First* 207)

any monkeys that had previously *walked* the earth

　　　　　　　　　　　　　　　　　(Koontz *Fear* 233)

the ghosts that *walked* this floor　　　(Hailey *Hotel* 97)

we *walk* him across the lawn　　(Grisham *Rainmaker* 233)

they *walked* the long, long hall to the back elevator

　　　　　　　　　　　　　　　　　(Steel *Paris* 37)

the young man who was walking or *being walked* by the beast

　　　　　　　　　　　　　　　　　(Block *Closet* 138)

⑤ 結果を表す表現

cry herself to sleep / talk me into leading this place / wait Mary out [= wait for Mary to go out] / laugh the actor off the stage / walk one's shoes to pieces

I *smiled* my okay.　　　　　　　　　(Dickey *Sister* 326)

I *laughed* my reply (笑って答えた)　　(Robbins *Stranger* 25)

⑥ その他

接頭辞による他動詞化

if he had *pre*deceased her...(彼女より先に死ぬ)

(Sanders *Luck* 277)

cf. *think the solution vs. *re*think the solution

9.5.2 自動詞化

① NP 削除

目的語が文脈から明らかな場合、また、動詞自身の意味から明らかな場合省かれる。

somehow, he had to *find out* φ　　　　(Sheldon *Naked* 69)

Lunatics rarely *kill* φ　　　　(Sheldon *Bloodline* 209)

He had *killed* φ for her, but he had *killed* φ for others, too.

(Sheldon *Rage* 335)

He was filled with such rage that he could have *killed* (this woman)

(Sheldon *Bloodline* 369)

If I were you I would *refuse* φ.　　　(Sheldon *Bloodline* 246)

He could not wait for them to *attack* φ　(Sheldon *Bloodline* 257)

he expected the novelist to be eccentric. But Mary had *disappointed* (Vic) in that regard ; he had been the most normal...neighbor.　　　　(Koontz *Murder* 226)

You'll hold the mortgage on the building and the land. You can't *lose* φ.　　　　(Sheldon *Stars* 53)

his son's fourth birthday, and we were going to take a boat trip to Kyron to *celebrate* φ　　　　(Sheldon *Other* 325)

If those are for the Red Cross...I already *gave* φ

(Sheldon *Other* 364)

we all *await* with baited breath　　　　(Archer *First* 33)

　　　　you're going to just *lay* back　　　　(Koontz *Fear* 212)
　　　　laying on his back　　　　(Block *Topless* 155)
② self 削除
　　　　identify < identify oneself
　　　　overwork / overeat / oversleep < {overwork / overeat / oversleep} oneself
　　　　dress / relax / adjust / wash / shave / drown < {dress / relax / adjust / wash / drown} oneself
　　　　mercifully he would *drown*　　　　(Hailey *Detective* 460)
　　　　Barbara *reached* to the dashboard controls (Koontz *Survivor* 174)
③ 前置詞の添加
　　　　visit *with* (19 c 半ばから AE でみられる) / meet *with* (AE) / raise *to* (AE) / hold *of* / tire *of*
　　　　give up NP > give up > give up *on* (an idea)
　　　　warn *against* education cuts (warn them of the danger / warn that S のように他動詞であったが 20 c 以降自動詞としても用いられる)
　　　　I finish *with* them.　　　　(Grisham *Rainmaker* 395)
　　　　I entered *into* a foyer.　　　　(Sanders *Secret* 48)
　　　　　cf. cope with > cope

9.5.3　能格動詞(ergative verb)・中間動詞(middle verb)

元来他動詞の目的語を主語として自動詞化する。修飾語を伴い現在形がふつうである。

　　　　The shoes all *sold* out. / She *interviews* (*photographs*) well. / This wine will *drink* well. / Do you *hurt*? / The car *handles* easily. / I don't *frighten* (*anger*) easily. / The door *opened* (*closed*). / The vase *broke*. / I don't *bruise* easily. / some wounds that don't *show* / the sink *cleans* easily / the cold lamb *eats* beautifully / your broken wrist will *heal*

strawberries *spoil* if left in water（AE で 1970 年頃受入れられる）

the boy's eyes were beginning to *fill* with fear　(Sheldon *Rage* 324)

what he did tell me has *checked out*, and you've proved it to be true

(Hailey *Detective* 398)

Freemantle was close enough to the microphone for his words to *carry*　　　　　　　　　　　　　　　(Hailey *Airport* 458)

Any meeting involving three hundred people would obviously cease to be secret the instant it *finished*　　　　　　(Hailey *Hotel* 321)

第 10 章 省略

10.1 代名詞・名詞の省略

（1） it の省略
① make / take / have は元来、直接目的節をとれなかったが、it を入れることでそれが可能となった。ところがそれが固定すると、とくに補語（形容詞や前置詞句）と動詞で、目的節をとれる1語の他動詞になったかのごとく it が略される。

make (it) certain that～ / make (it) sure that～ / take (it) *into account* that～ / have (it) *in common* that～ / take (it) *for granted* that～ / bear (it) *in mind* that～

 cf. depend upon it that S

② 慣用表現、非人称主語の it はしばしば口語で省略される。
もっともふつうの動詞の一致は主語と（他の言語では目的語ととも）である。英語では主語との一致が唯一なので動詞にその一致のマークがある時にその主語 it を省略することができる。

(it) serves you right / (it) looks like rain / (it) suits me / (it) seems good / (it is) no wonder he did it / (it is) no use crying / (it is) nice to meet you

How fortunate (it is) that we met

(2) I の省略

文脈から復元しやすいために起こる。

(I'm) Glad to see you.

(I) Hope to see you again.

Are you sticking to the schedule? — Sure am.

一般に主語位置に下記の条件下で省略が起こる。

① 主節で(従節では不可。*I believe ϕ must do it)

② 平叙文で(疑問文には起こらない。*Can ϕ do it? *What shall ϕ do?)。

③ 話題化が起こっている文では起こらない(*The poem, ϕ repeated to them)。

④ 否定語などによる倒置文でも起こらない(*Never have ϕ dreamed of it)。

⑤ くだけた文体、話しことば、日記などで起こりやすい。

(3) you の省略

(Do you) care to join us for a meal?

(Do you) like it?

(Have you) understood?

(4) what の省略

口語のとくに the problem / question is で始まる文で(AE, BE)起こる。

[What$_i$ the problem is t$_i$] is that no one can meet after 6 pm > [The problem] is that S > *The problem is* is that S

   cf. The thing is, is that S

My real feeling is, is that S

The strange thing was, is that S

(5) 直接目的語の省略

2つの目的語があるとき通例は間接目的語が削除されるが、文脈が明らかなときは直接目的語も省略されうる。動詞は tell, show が多い。

Why didn't you tell me?
Anne told him.　　　　　　　　　　　　(Sheldon *Bloodline* 31)
We're going to show them.　　　　　　(Sheldon *Stars* 349)
And yet Elizabeth had to know (more).
　　　　　　　　　　　　　　　　　　(Sheldon *Bloodline* 381)
"So what kind of doctor are you?" I told her.
　　　　　　　　　　　　　　　　　　(Cornwell *Unnatural* 226)
"Your name." I told her.　　　　　　(Cornwell *Unnatural* 287)

直接目的語が略され自動詞化することについては 9.5.2 参照。

10.2　動詞・助動詞の省略

(1) 動詞の省略

① 動作動詞 (go / come / be) の省略は AE の口語の特色である。これは ScE、IrE から来たものかもしれない (cf. Murder will out.)。これは to be にも及ぶ。

The cat wants φ in / out.
Larry wanted her φ with him　　　　(Sheldon *Other* 387)
I ordered him (to go) to Frankfurt
　　　　　　　　　　　　　　　　　　(Sheldon *Windmills* 419)
　　cf. I want her examined　　　　　(Sheldon *Stars* 178)

② 空所化 (gapping)

Mary likes John and John φ Kitty.
Mary plays tennis with John and Jim φ with Harriet.
The trouble would annoy May and it φ me, too.

（２） 動詞句（VP）削除

Who is *singing* today? May is ϕ.

Anyone who can ϕ should *see me*.

I'll *try it* if I must ϕ.

I have not *written it* but he will ϕ.

 cf. I would *like him to eat* fruit more than I would ϕ cookies（今西・浅野（1990:300））――擬似空所化（pseudo-gapping）の例

  Move the car. AE: I {have / might / did / am}.

       BE: I {have done / might do / did do / am doing}.

（３） 助動詞削除

We *have been* to Paris and he ϕ to London.

Mary *must have arrived there* and Bill ϕ, too.

（４） その他

① (It's) been a nice week so far.

He could guess *what* ϕ about   (Steel *Paris* 238)

② who / what / how のあとで動詞の省略が起こる。最初 AE で、のち BE でも起こる。

What ϕ to do?

Who ϕ to ask?

③ as far as (be concerned)（⇒ 接続詞の前置詞化）

She...had her father's genes, at least *as far as* skiing (is concerned)

            (Steel *Ghost* 314)

 cf. You've done such a splendid job so far as an investigator（～がやる程度まで） (Sanders *Puzzle* 194)

10.3　接続詞の省略

（1）　that の省略

that の省略はとくに口語でひんぱんに起こる。

① 動詞や be＋形容詞の後ろで。

believe / presume / suppose / think / be afraid / be sure / be glad とくに think / know / say / hope / tell / guess のあとで省略される。that が保たれるのは formal、省略されるのは informal speech である。

（ⅰ）　that を省略するのがふつうのもの：wish / hope / it is time / I'd rather

（ⅱ）　that を伴う方がふつうのもの：agree / assume / conceive / maintain / suggest / state / prove / feel / be delighted / be aware / be sad

formal な advise / suggest / intend などのあとでは that を保つ。

（ⅲ）　いずれも可能なもの：consider / hear / say / tell / know / see / understand / find / expect

She said φ she thought φ she had seen him before.
　　　　　　　　　　　　　　　　　　　　　(Sanders *Risk* 164)
　　cf.　I know for a fact φ he went to Noose's house
　　　　　　　　　　　　　　　　　　　　　(Grisham *Time* 289)
　　...make up her mind *that* this was what she was going to do
　　　　　　　　　　　　　　　　　　　　　(Koontz *Intensity* 213)
　　I take it φ this is your first baby　(Sheldon *Rage* 239)

② 仮定法は that をふつう伴う。demand, suggest のあとの that は省略されるが、仮定法がつづくときは省略されにくい。

I demand *that* he *be* here.
　　cf. She suggested he go on about his life.　　(Steel *Ghost* 79)
　　　　(Steel *Ghost* における省略はみな suggest の後に限られている。)

③　so の後ろで

He was *so* tired φ he could not eat.

He moved forward so φ he could hear better.

You were so quiet φ I thought you had forgotten I was with you
　　　　　　　　　　　　　　　　　(Robbins *Stranger* 120)

④　同格節（idea, feeling, fear などのあと）としての that の省略。主節と従節の境界を示すような分裂文、it is の後、補語とも起こる。

I have no idea φ he will come today.

I have a feeling φ we're going to be good friends.

It was Mellis φ Eve was concerned about.

What is it φ you wish me to do?

It was Allerton φ I was interested in　　(Christie *Curtain* 127)

It's Roberta φ you have to worry about　　(Robbins *Stallion* 333)

It is {a pity / a wonder / strange} φ...

It was no wonder φ her smile was glazed　　(Sanders *Risk* 149)

The good news is φ you should have...

The stupid part is φ I sent it to him.

The truth is φ John has no friends.

make the claim (assumption, assertion) / make a guess / come to the conclusion / make a rule のあとでも that は省略が可能である。

There is some speculation φ the trial will be postponed
　　　　　　　　　　　　　　　　　(Grisham *Time* 340)

there were roumors φ ABC wanted to pick him up for a nationwide
audience　　　　　　　　　　　　　　　　　(Koontz *Face* 17)
　　cf. chances are φ such a man is...　　(Forsyth *Jackal* より)
⑤　関係副詞としての that の省略
　　on the day φ Robert arrived　　　　　(Sheldon *Doomsday* 125)
⑥　発話様態動詞 (manner-of-speaking verb)
　　chortle, scream, shout, lisp, mutter, murmur, snort, rejoice, whine,
　　whisper などのあとでは that があるのが原則である。
　　She whispered over and over *that* she loved him...
　　　　　　　　　　　　　　　　　　　　　　(Klavan *Crime* 234)
　　She snarled *that* her son hadn't gotten in...　　(Cornwell)
⑦　NP からの外置の場合は省略されない。
　　A proposal had been made *that* the possibility be considered of...
　　The book (that) Kay wrote arrived. → The book arrived (*that)
　　Kay wrote.
⑧　the fact / reason is のあとは that がないのが原則である。
⑨　that のうしろが full NP (the man, Jim...) のときよりも人称代名詞
　　のときに省略される傾向が強い。
　　it's not likely φ *he*'ll be a nobody again　　(Koontz *Face* 81)
　　to an extent φ *she* had never done before　　(Koontz *Face* 149)
　　　cf. he announced *to the crowd* φ these silly fools wanted chef
　　　　 salads　　　　　　　　　　　　　　　(Grisham *Time* 112)
　　　　　 He told me *Tuesday* φ there was too much damage
　　　　　　　　　　　　　　　　　　　　　　(Grisham *Time* 221-2)
⑩　utterance verb 'say' などのあとで時制の不一致のとき that を使うの
　　は不自然である (Givón (1993:20-21))。
　　I said (?that) you're coming.
⑪　主語の位置では略さない (*That) the world is flat is obvious.

⑫ 補文の内容が重要なことをのべているときの方が that は保持されやすい。

He mentioned { that the king had died. / Jim was coming for tea. }

⑬ 主節と従節の関係 (discourse factors)
　（ⅰ） 主節の主語と同一指示の代名詞主語が従節にある時、that が省略されるのが 88.9％、されないのが 11.1％ である。従節にそのような代名詞がなく、full NP 主語のときは that が省略されるのが 79.2％、されないのが 20.7％ である。

また、
　（ⅱ） 従節の主語が definite であるとき
　（ⅲ） 主節または従節の主語が 1 / 2 人称代名詞のとき
　（ⅳ） 主節の主語が I / you のときに
省略が好まれる傾向がある。

⑭ 主節に助動詞、間接目的語、副詞などが現れるとき that が好まれる（千葉 1995）。

I will decide that〜 / I decided 〜

warn {him / the US} that S

I argued with Bill *(that) he should…

*I believe *strongly* φ he is…

Jim believes, but Kay doesn't, *(that) Mary is smart.

It was apparent yesterday *(that)…

I doubt *very much* that〜　　　　　　　（Sanders *Risk* 77）

…suggested *very strongly* that Noose leave the trial here

（Grisham *Time* 289）

⑮ 史的には that の省略は Late ME 〜 EModE で急速に増す。特に（ⅰ）従節の主語が代名詞のとき（ⅱ）V と that の間に介在する要素がないとき（ⅲ）口語体のときにそうである。

1350-1400　14%

1640-1710　70%

⑯　become convinced / be certain のような断定的述語(assertive predicate)のあとでは that が省略されるのに対し、非断定的述語(non-assertive predicate)のあとでは that が保たれる。しかし

 cf. Is it at all possible φ you might see me sometime today?

(Sanders Puzzle 159)

⑰　register factors

会話では that が省略されるのが原則であるが、学術的な散文体では逆に that を保つ傾向が強い。

⑱　that が保たれる場合：

 (ⅰ)　等位接続された構造で(agree that S and that S)

 (ⅱ)　主節が受動態のとき(I was told that S)

  it is believed by Jim *(that) S

  it is believed (that) S

   cf. it may be claimed φ the letters are...

(Sanders Risk 75)

(2) and の省略

A, B, C の語句をならべるとき口語では A と B の間の and を用いないのがふつう(Bauer 1993)。

He had a moustache, φ glasses and was wearing a blue pullover.

(3) as の省略

so と呼応し、to 不定詞を伴うとき非常にまれであるが、古くはこれがふつうだった。

be so relieved φ to... / φ long as you like

I'll be back φ fast as I can　　　　　(Koontz *Moon* 397)

φ far as I'm concerned　　　　　　(Archer *Matter* 196)

φ soon's [= as soon as] I heard her story I went right out

(Robbins *Lady* 94)

 cf. φ matter of fact, I haven't even read it at the time

(Robbins *Merchants* 77)

（4）if の省略

 even φ should one have the misfortune to encounter bad weather

(Archer *Hiccup* 124)

10.4　前置詞の省略

（1）時の表現

非常に広範に起こり、前置詞を伴わなければならないケースの方が少なくなってきているといってもいいほどである。

① this / that / last / next / every を伴うとき、すでに副詞化した yesterday, today, tomorrow などは必ず前置詞を落とす。

next morning / next weekend / that evening / every winter / last summer vacation / last term / late (early) Monday afternoon / these days (cf. (in) those days) / Thursday night (morning)

this weekend we cured

one February it came to an abrupt end

last season he had had several spectacular wins

(Hailey *Wheels* 202)

ただし、「この特定の」の意味の this のときは落ちない。

on *this* evening / on *this* morning (she walked to her office)

 cf. nine on Sunday night

   on that November evening

② 曜日と。BE では口語で省略される。AE ではしばしば曜日を伴う時も省略される。

I'll phone you (on) Monday / (on) Friday evening / (on) tomorrow night.

I work Sundays.

I used to work weekends as a tour guide.

 cf. he worked there summers

③ 前後に修飾語を伴う「特定の日」。疑問詞と。

(on) the following morning / day / week

(in) the previous winter

(in) the June before last

what time are you starting?

φ the night of the general's murder

φ The morning of Mrs Cooper's release she telephoned Jennifer

         (Sheldon *Rage* 185)

φ the day of her graduation (Sheldon *Bloodline* 167)

She saw him in her Latin class φ the day the term began

         (Sheldon *Other* 33)

④ 期間を表す for の省略

stay (for) two weeks / (for) a lot of time

He lay awake (for) the rest of the night

speak (for) two minutes

He studied it (for) a moment

He is not close to anyone φ his entire life

⑤ その他

I saw the monkey at the window φ the first time

         (Koontz *Fear* 209)

(2) VI+P

if I fail (in) your course / suffer (from) rheumatism / go out (of) the room / stare out the window / wheel out the cart

cope（with）（BE では 1930〜）／ there's no place for him to go（to）
all the women working（on）the streets（Sheldon *Doomsday* 346）
Jennifer was out（of）the door　　　（Sheldon *Rage* 169, 413）
protest（against）some actions by the US（20 c 初めから AE で）
Nominal syllables contribute（to）a single tone bearing unit
traveling first class　　　　　　　　　（Archer *Principle* 146）
To begin φ Richard allocated one afternoon a week to researching the feud...　　　　　　　　　　　　　　（Archer *Prod* 168）

(3) VT 構文で

prevent us（from）going out（BE に多い）
it will not stop you φ concentrating properly on〜
keep A（from）-ing
stop me φ seeing what he looked like
　　　　　　　　　　　　　　　　　　（Archer *Cristina* 209）
have {difficulty ／ a hard time ／ fun} φ doing it
have no problem φ saying that S
have no trouble φ picking him up
has no business φ working in this hospital
　　　　　　　　　　　　　　　　　　（Sheldon *Nothing* 134）
have the most difficult time φ choosing something to wear
spend time（in, on）studying
waste time（in, on）doing
The afternoon was spent φ listening to a series of complaints
　cf.　took a long time to like people　　（Archer *Prod* 191）
they could have fun φ doing macabre　　（Block *Closet* 99）

(4) NP 修飾の不定詞句中

文脈から明らかな場合にしばしばみられる。名詞は道具や場所を表すものが多い。

a ball pen to write (with) / the place to look (at) / Do you have any place to go (to) / a comfortable place to work (at) or to live (in) / it's a perfect place for you to rest (at) / a place to sleep there was no one to listen φ　　　　　　　(Steel *Ghost* 356)

 cf. I have nothing to be afraid of / I have some business to attend to / I have a meeting to go to / there is no one to go with / there is nothing to prepare for

(5) Adj (Adv)＋P

① *absent from* の from を落とし、前置詞のように 'without' の意味で AE で 20 c 半ばから使われ始める。意味や構文の似ている without, lacking, missing の影響(Slotkin 1994)。最初 AE で始まり、1944 年、法律文に現れ、1970 年代に広がる (AE, BE)。

Absent a good name for it, we term it...

That's the Stallion [＝car], *absent* its body.
          (Robbins *Stallion* 176)

walls were *absent* the expected photographs of himself with politicians or celebrities   (Cornwell *Potter's* 231)

② *according to*

まれに to を落とす。

In the taxi...the clock showed 6 pence extra ; he tipped *according*. (SOD)

③ *regardless* (*of*)

Though my voice was vanishing I struggled on *regardless*.

But the Germans never change. "*Regardless*," Jacques said. I feel I must do something...   (Robbins *Pred* 81)

He decided to go ahead *regardless*. (Forsyth *Jackal* 301)

④ *due* (*to*)

All I want is to get the money that is *due* φ me

(Robbins *Pred* 56)

the forty dollars…that is *due* φ him　　(Koontz *Intensity* 117)

It would give her status, the respect and deference *due* φ the wife of a famous scientist　　(Sanders *Pleasures* 302)

⑤ *near* のあとで *to* が省略される。

ただし nearer to / nearest to the house

⑥ その他

alongside (of) / inside (of) a month / outside (of) the Hermitage Museum / I must discuss business outside (of) office hours.

inside of 'within' (AE)

　　cf. outside of 'outside' (AE で) BE は of なし。

(6) その他

① (by) way of / (in) spite of / (in) back of / (for) sake of / (of) course など時折口語で見られる。

② a couple (of) [əv] > [ə] > φ　(cf. coupla)

a variety (of)

③ What do you mean (by) A?

④ 補文標識 (complementizer) 'for'

All they want is φ people to check in, check out and pay the bill; that's all　　(Hailey *Hotel* 41)

⑤ For a while I considered going back to university, then decided *not* φ. (代不定詞 to の略。しかし先行詞は -ing)　　(Hailey *Hotel* 72)

⑥ we're short φ four pages of copy　　(Robbins)

⑦ My wife was late φ getting back home.

⑧ 「色」「大きさ」「形」「高さ」「長さ」などを示す名詞と。

φ What color is it?

a girl φ my age

He's φ the same height as me.

ϕ What shoe size is she?

a swimming pool ϕ the size of a lake

⑨ way

(in) a certain way / (in) this way / (in) the wrong way

He didn't do it the way we did.

GE did business ϕ the Japanese way.

10.5 冠詞の省略

圧倒的に the の省略が多い。

（1）補語の名詞として become や as のあとで

become (a) reality / seem (a) fair comment

I was ϕ {captain / president} of the football team.

He was elected ϕ {chair / president}.

He is regarded as ϕ role model.

（2）kind 句で

He is not the kind of ϕ person to help us.

（3）時間の表現

all ϕ evening / all ϕ year / (a) quarter to ten / in (the) winter / all (the) summer

ϕ day before yesterday　　　　　　　　（Robbins *Stallion* 310）

They were married on April ϕ first.　　　（Steel *Ghost* 385）

（4）ϕ Following is the list of some of the organizations

（Sheldon *Dreams* 338）

ϕ Same for a rich corporation　　　（Grisham *Rainmaker* 545）

（5）慣用的ないい方

(the) point is, S / (the) fact is... / (the) trouble is... / (the) Government / the police（警察全体）〜 police（個々の警察官）/

when φ term ended / on (the) radio / go to (the) university / to tell the truth > truth to tell / in (the) case of / (the) measles

φ fact was augmented by fiction　　　　　(Archer *Matter* 14)
φ Deceased was poisoned　　　　　(Christie *Curtain* 195)
φ Best thing in the world...　　　　　(Grisham *Runaway* 166)
φ Same to you　　　　　(Cornwell *Unnatural* 92)
The cops got φ angrier the more she cried
　　　　　(Grisham *Runaway* 229)
Dialects of a language tend to differ φ more from one another the more remote they are from one another geographically
　　　　　(Romaine 1994: 2)

(6) Prince, Minister, Major の the の省略はとくに AE で
　　Mary Jones, *a* bored housewife → bored housewife Mary Jones
　　Dr Smith, Head of the English Department → Head of English Department Dr Smith

(7) とくに geopolitical な語やアクロニム (acronym) で (AE)
　　the Ukraine > Ukraine
　　the Japanese agree > Japanese agree
　　the UN is waiting > UN is waiting

(8) その他
　　brief exposure to φ *sun*　　　　　(Koontz *Fear* 22)

第11章　一致

11.1　主語と動詞の一致

① 集合名詞と動詞

一般的にいうと集合名詞は単数動詞と一致する傾向を強めている。とくに BE ではそうである。

  government BE では「イギリス政府」のとき複数。他の政府は単数扱い。AE では単数扱い。

  committee, team 単数扱いが増えている。とくに BE で。

  group, class 単、複いずれも。

直前の名詞で左右されることがある。

the majority of *the charge* is

the majority of *criminals* are

the police want to talk to him（AE）

The police were searching for an unnamed Englishman（BE）

One couple were already seated at the table.　　（Archer *4th* 351）

② 不定代名詞

 （ⅰ）none

  none は複数扱いがふつうで単数扱いは 17 c 以降まれとなったが

20cになると依然複数扱いが多いが単数が増えてきた。

「物」のときは単数が多いが、「人」のときは単数、複数いずれも。AEでは単数が多い（Brown Corpusでは63％）。

None of them *are* / *is* here.

None of us *needs*... (BE単数扱いが多い)

None of the people *is*...　　　　　　(Sheldon *Morning* 268)

None of the networks *was*...　　　　　(Archer *4th* 242)

none of them *are*...　　　　　　　　(Archer *Thieves* 149)

(ii)　neither / either　単、複数いずれでも呼応する。

{Neither / Either} of my friends {*has* / *have*}...

③　there構文

thereが主語と感じられているので動詞につづく名詞の数とはしばしば不一致で単数扱い。

④　what節の一致

動詞は単、複いずれでも呼応するが単数の方が多い。しかし、補語の複数や文脈中に複数を示唆する語句があるとき複数で呼応する。

What is right *is* right.

What were truths *are* truths.

What I want *are* details.

there *are* what appear to be veins that contain a green liquor

(Sheldon *Doomsday* 88)

What's fascinating *are* these dark spots...　　　(Archer)

⑤　either A or B, neither A nor B, A or Bと動詞

AはBと文法上の等価物なので動詞は直前のBと一致するのが原則だが、全体がandで結ばれた句であるかのごとく複数動詞で呼応することがある。とくにneither A or B, neither A nor Bで多くみられ、either A or Bでは少ない。一方A or Bも複数対応が多い。

Neither John nor James *have* dealt with it.

There *have* been neither a fire engine or an ambulance.

Neither Adam nor Robin *were* able to make out where the bid had come from.　　　　　　　　　　　　　　　(Archer *Matter* 358)

neither of them *was*　　　　　　　　(Archer *Thieves* 33, 438)

neither Craig nor I *knows* you're seeing the other one

　　　　　　　　　　　　　　　　　　(Block *Closet* 155)

11.2　呼応

(1) everyone / anybody

everyone / anybody を they で受けるのは AE ではすでに 1940 年ごろ確立しているが今日なお反対する意見が根強くある。

1985 年の数字によれば意見は 5 分 5 分で分かれている (AE) が、1990 年の数字 (AE) では

he	they	he or she	she	one
34%	32%	22%	8%	4%

となっている。

Everyone likes pizza, doesn't he? (don't they?)

1998 年ではあらゆる場合でふつう。

(2) one

BE では one で呼応することが一般的だが AE では he で呼応することも同じくらい多い (one 54% vs. he 46%)。

(3) 照応 (anaphora)

原則として従節＋主節の構文 (periodic sentence) で、従節中の名詞/代名詞は主節中の代名詞/名詞と同じ内容を指す。Pron...N 型はジャーナリズムで好まれる。

When *Mary* arrives send *her* in.

When *she* arrives send *Mary* in.

Tired as *she* was *Mary* continued to work.

As *he* reads *it* the *reader* understands *the text*.

As *he* passed the open compartment, *the man* smiled

(Archer *Matter* 328)

As Romanov moved toward *him*, *Adam* took a pace backward from the streetcar lines to allow the streetcar to pass between them

(Archer *Matter* 162)

 cf. Diplomats who have known *him* agree that *Gromyko* has a prodigious mind...

一方、主節＋従節の構文 (loose sentence) では主節の名詞と従節の代名詞は同じ内容を指すが、主節の代名詞と従節の名詞は同じ内容を指せない。

Send *Mary* in when *she* arrives.

*Send *her* in when *Mary* arrives.

11.3 kind / sort と this / that

1940年ごろの AE では these *kind* of gloves は口語では受け入れられ始めたが書きことばでは問題ありとされた。

 several kinds of trees

第 12 章　語順

12.1　従節の中の倒置

　主節と補文のちがいの 1 つは補文ではあまり異なる語順を用いないことである。
(1)　従節内で見られる否定の副詞や場所を表す前置詞句のうしろの倒置
　　　It seemed to Susan that *no sooner* did Robert return from one assignment than he was sent away on another
　　　　　　　　　　　　　　　　　　　　　　(Sheldon *Doomsday* 136)
　　　You're here...because *in this room* are some of the greatest bankers in the world　　　(Sheldon *Bloodline* 248)
(2)　the question のあと
　　　The question is where the hell has he gone...
　　　The question is, are you speaking the truth ?
　　　　　　　　　　　　　　　　　　　　　　(Christie *Curtain* 197)
　　　"The question is," she said..., "are you big enough to forgive him ?
　　　　　　　　　　　　　　　　　　　　　　(Steel *Paris* 264)
(3)　ask / wonder などにつづく疑問文で
　　　AE では最近くだけた口語でしばしば起こる。She asked *could she*

go to the movies.

I asked *could I* wear it? (Block *Hit* 18)

People asked me how well *did I* know Hilton.

So I keep asking myself why *could she* defect?
(Archer *Matter* 115)

I...ask Chiquita why *was she* in my personal life
(Dickey *Friends* 147)

I demanded *did he* really believe the Body of Christ was present on the altar at the consecration. (Rice *Vampire* 57)

she figured out who was who and why *was he* here
(Grisham *Runaway* 414)

What I don't know is why *did he* kill her? (Parker *Vices* 302)

Now they would want to know...how she felt now that they were gone,...and how *could she* explain it. (Steel *Paris* 216)

He knew how serious *was the job of an officer of the law*
(Forsyth *Jackal* 311)

She went upstairs...wondering how, eventually, *was she* going to tell him the truth about her. (Steel *Gift* 128)

I thought why *should I* (Sanders *Risk* 218)

1998年Michiganの学生によると80％ぐらいがI wonder why *did Sally* leave? を拒絶している。

What I figured...is why *would you* be coming here?
(Block *Kipling* 165)

What I said is what *did we* ever witness?
(Block *Kipling* 165)

BelfastEでは従節の倒置(VS)はふつうだが、V = Aux / have / be に限られ本動詞では許されない。

*They asked me *went I* to the party.

第 13 章 語形

13.1 名詞

（1）単複同形

重量、距離などを表す場合

two pound ／ twenty foot ／ two mile

（2）不規則複数形と規則複数形で意味が異なる場合

wolves〜wolfs ［＝aggressive men］

mice〜mouses ［＝Mickey Mouses］

geese〜gooses ［＝foolish persons］(cf. silly gooses ／ Mother Gooses)

oxen〜oxes ［＝stupid persons］

lives〜still lifes

dice(さいころ)〜dies ［＝stamps］

（3）talk about $\begin{cases} \text{a million anythings} \\ \text{nothings} \end{cases}$

（4）揺れる複数

① formula ＞ formulae〜formulas

（formulas はすでに AE 1936、1966 の調査で受入れられている）

datum / medium はしばしば複数形 data / media で使われるのでそれらの複数形が単数形と考えられ、{data / the mass media} is のように使われる。その場合複数形は datas / medias となることがある。しかし data are もよく用いられる。

② -ths [θ] ～[ð]

mouths / truths / paths / moths は BE では [θ] を好むが AE では [ð] も用いられる。

ただし deaths は [θ] のみである。

③ -fs～-ves

wharfs (BE)～wharves (AE)

BE でも -ves が地歩を固めつつある。

AE のリアルタイム	1936	1983
handkerchief	s～vz	s
hoof	s～vz	s～vz
scarf	vz～s	s がふつう
staff	s～vz	s～vz
dwarf	s	s～vz[注1]
roof	s	s

注1 BE では s が多かったが Tolkien が vz を使ってから増えた。

13.2 形容詞/副詞

(1) 一般に -er / -est よりも more / most が好まれる傾向がある。とくに2音節以上の語ではそうである。ただし -y に終わる形容詞は -er / -est が圧倒的に多い。

most common / more often / more senseless / more sure

I'm *sorriest* about Abby　　　　　　　(Cornwell *All* 382)

New York Times	1900	1989
-y に終わる形容詞の -er / -est	66.2%	82.8%

(2) more / most を好む傾向は 1 音節語にも及ぶ。

　　most just / most real〜realest
　　more right　cf. righter, rightest
　　(be) more like (you)　　　　　　　　　　　(Simon)

(3) true の比較級は more を、最上級は -est を好む。
　　more true / truest

(4) badder, baddest は 'tough' の意味のときに、
　　less, lesser「価値の少ない」の意味で使われる。

(5) 複合語の well-known も better-known よりも more well-known が好まれる。

(6) most {unique / perfect / complete} は 1970 年の AE ではまだ 7 割近く反対であったが、しばしば使われる。

13.3　動詞

(1) 規則変化を好むようになった動詞: family resemblance(タイプの頻度や音声的類似)のゆえに規則化しやすい。とくに①のように母音交替のないものは規則化しやすい。

　① smelt > smeled(AE)(BE では[t]も) / spelt > spelled(AE) / dwelt > dwelled / spoilt > spoiled　(AE)(AE, BE いずれも[t]も) / burnt > burned / learnt / learned(過去形に AE, BE いずれも[t]も) / earnt > earned

　② dreamt > dreamed (AE)(BE では [t] も。過去分詞はとくに [t])

knelt > kneeled（AE）（BE では［t］も）

leapt > leaped（AE）（BE では［t］も）

（２）揺れる動詞

① 原形と同形の過去形と規則形で揺れる。

lit〜lighted ／ wet〜wetted ／ fit〜fitted ／ bet〜betted ／ quit〜quitted ／ input〜inputted ／ wed〜wedded

②

		AE	BE
show	過去	-ed	-ed
	過去分詞	-n〜-ed	-n
wake	過去	woke〜-d	woke〜-d
	過去分詞	woken〜-d	woken〜-d （ただし woke *up*）
dive		-d［AE では dove も］	-d

③ 意味、統語的制限を受けるもの

hanged（絞首刑にする）〜hang

proved〜proven（過去分詞）　限定（attributive）用法のときは前者が好まれる。AE では 1938 年の調査では問題ありであったが 1969 年においては 73％が容認している。

drunk〜drunken　前者は叙述（predicative）用法で、後者は限定用法で好まれる。

bereaved（死なれた）〜bereft（奪われた）

④ 複合語では規則形を用いるのが原則

joy-ride > joy-rided　*-rode（車をのりまわす）

high-stick > high-sticked *-stuck（アイスホッケー用語）

nosedived ／ troubleshooted

⑤ drag の過去形は drug がよりふつうになりつつある（AE）

⑥ broadcast　〜-ed

⑦ input ／ output　〜-ed

第 14 章 語彙

14.1 語彙

(1) 概論

英語の語彙はおおざっぱにみると、OE では 35,000、このうち 60%は ME に入ると失われ、ME では 45,000、EModE では 125,000、PE では 62 万以上(OED の第 2 版)あるといわれている。

英語の語彙は、歴史的にみると (ⅰ)借入による増大が圧倒的で、(ⅱ)造語、(ⅲ)語形成によることはそれに比べると弱かった。しかし、とくに今世紀に入ると、(ⅰ)によらず、自己生産によっていろいろなコミュニケーションの要求に答えようとするのがふつうになってきた。

今日の新造語(neologism)では複合(compounding)、接辞添加(affixation)がもっともふつうで、これに転換がつづく。借入、短化、blend などは頻度が低い。

ある数字によれば OE の語彙の 3% が借入なのに
PE の語彙の 70% が借入である。

ある数字によればこの 50 年の新しい語彙の数は

複合 36%

接辞添加 27%

ゼロ派生　　17%

短化(back formation, clips, acronym)　　9%

blending　　6%

14.2 借入

① 英語の借入による語彙の増大化は ME で頂点に達し、ルネッサンス以降は急激に減ってきている。20ｃになるとさらにそうで、医学など一部のものを除き L からの借入も止め、たとえば、1970 年代までの 4,000〜5,000 ほどの新語のうち借入によるものは 6%ほどにすぎない。今日では俗語、口語からの語彙を教養ある人達が使ったり taboo 視されていた 4 文字語(four-letter word)を TV、舞台でしばしば使うようなことで語彙を豊かにしている。若い人は「はやりことば」を使って up to date 感の印象をつくる(cf. great → brill → cool あるいは wicked)。

② 借入の段階(Cannon 1994)
　（ⅰ）第1段階は新しく入ってきた語は斜字体または引用符でそれとわかる表示をつける。
　（ⅱ）第2段階は、音声、文法、意味上の adaptation の初期段階にあって借入源の書記法に従う。
　（ⅲ）第3段階は、辞書に収録され、耳にしても理解しうる。接辞添加、複合等によりいくぶん生産的となる。
　（ⅳ）最終段階は元来の意味と違った意味をもち、生産的となる。

③ 借入の動機づけ
　（ⅰ）新しい cultural item(外国の技術・宗教・地勢・動物・植物など)にふれる必要性。
　（ⅱ）prestige(pig—pork, cow—beef)あるいは教養のあるようにみせるため(英語の penname に対してフランス語 nom de plume)。

④ 借入の条件
　（ⅰ）辞書項目が借入されないと文法形態素は借入されない。小範疇語の借入は抵抗される（ただし英語の they, though は例外）。
　（ⅱ）拘束形は完全な（独立）語の一部としてのみ借入される（-able, -ette）。のち自由形＋拘束形のように再解釈され、拘束形は生産的になったり、非生産的になったりする。
　（ⅲ）N の方が V/A よりも借入されやすい。とくに V は直接借入されにくい（ただし、ON get, take ／ F desire などの例もある）。それは N が数多いこと、文法構造に適応しやすいためである。
　（ⅳ）屈折接辞の借入は派生接辞の借入のあとに起こる。事実、前者の借入はきわめてまれである。
　（ⅴ）頻度の高い基本語は借入されにくい。
　　　1) 代名詞　2) 低い数字　3) 血縁語　4) 身体の名称
　　　5) 基本動詞(go, eat, be)　6) 基本形容詞(black, red, big, small, old)　7) 自然現象(rain, sun, night)　8) 文法語(if, this, and)

英語に入ってきた品詞別借入語の割合

	名詞	形容詞	動詞	副詞	間投詞	その他
中国語	83%	15%	1.9%	0.1%	0.3%	0.6%
ドイツ語	88%	9.2%	1.1%	0.16%	0.38%	1.16%
スペイン語	88.2%	11.1%		0.7%		
日本語	91%	8.2%		0.4%		0.4%

⑤ 借入語の取り扱い
　言語によって扱いを異にする。（ⅰ）のようにそのまま借入するよりも（ⅱ）のように借入した言語の組織にあうよう改変されるのがふつうである。
　（ⅰ）そのまま借入する場合
　　1) ME には語中に [v] があったが語頭の [v] は F 借入語(value,

virgin)による。また [ʒ] は、本来語の zi > ʒ の変化の他 EModE の F 借入語(measure, leisure)の [ʒ] による。

最近の AE、一部 BE にみられるようになった子音結合 [ʃp ʃt ʃl ʃm ʃn ʃv ʃw] はドイツ語や Yiddish からの借入による (spiel, schnauzer, schlep, Schweppes)。

2) F には元来欠けていた [ŋ] を、英語の -ing [iŋ] 借入語に負うている (smoking [= 〜jacket] living [= 〜room])。

F で -ing が生産的となる (lifting[= face-lift], brushing[= blow-dry])。

3) ドイツ語には -e, -er, -en などの複数接辞があるが、最近は英語の -s の影響でまれな -s をつける傾向がある (Tests, Hotels, Kameras)。

(ii) 借入した言語にあわせる場合

1) (ア)英語にない複数は英語の複数形を拡大する (data > datas)。

日本語では N を借りて -suru (light verb) をつけて V を生む (doraibu-suru)。

(イ)ドイツ語には -e, -er, -en などの複数接辞があるが、借入語にどれかを付与しようとする (Film-e / Pilot-en)。

ドイツ語の格接辞 Nom / Acc(-ϕ, -en), G(-es, -en), D(-(e), -en) があるが借入語には添加されないのが原則。まれに Tents [= tent's] のような例も起こる。

なお Rus も借入語には格接辞を与えない。

(ウ)F には 2 つの性があるので借入語にも性を与えるが、ほとんど男性 Msc(western [= film], zip, jazz, weekend) である。しかしドイツ語は男性 Msc、女性 Fmn、中性 Neut のいずれかにふりわける。ただし、Curry, Yoghurt のように Msc, Neut で揺れるものもある。

Msc	Fmn	Neut
Cocktail	Yacht	Bridge
Best seller	Lady	Quiz

2) 英語にはFの鼻母音 [ã, ɛ̃] がなく、ドイツ語の [y] がないので

　(ア) 自国語音に近い音で置換する

　　　G　muesli ＞ E　[mjuːzli, -sli]

　(イ) 原語音をまねて「外国語」のように発音する。prestigious と考えられているときとくにそうである。

　　　F　genre ＞ E　[ʒɑ̃ːrə] 〜 [ʒɑ̃ːnrə]

⑥ 最近の借入語

　(i) 今世紀に入ってきた借入語は

　1) 最近 25 年 (1963-88) の借入語の 1 位〜5 位は

　　F(254 語)　Sp(80)　Jap(80)　It(75)　L(73),（以下, G, Gk, Yid, Rus, Ch とつづく）

　　OED の補遺版によると借入語の数は

1900-1930	68
1940	29
1950	62
1960-1985	138

　2) 例

　　F　actualité / art deco / nouvelle cuisine / au pair / montage / boutique

　　英国と距離的に近いこと、学校で F を教育すること、文化、エンターテイメント、couture, cuisine, fashion などのすぐれていることから。

Jap　（⇒次節参照）
Sp　　bonanza / chicano
L　　　科学、政治、哲学などいろいろな方面から。
Gk　　topos / logos / techno-
　　　新しい学問語として造語されることが多い。
Sw　　orienteering
Norw　ombudsman
Esk　　anorak
Rus　　perestroika
G　　　科学、政治、哲学などいろいろな方面から
　　　Auschluss / dunk / kattck / kltch / Vaseline

(ⅱ) 最近の日本語借入

1) 日本語の、とくに AE への流入は、文化接触、人事交流などもあってかなりの数にのぼる。経済的隆盛ゆえ 20 c 後半からいろいろな面から入って来る。

1892 年の数字では全借入語 13,018 のうち 3,797(L)、2,617(F)、716(It) に対して 22 位の 27 のみであった。

Cannon(1987) によれば 1 位の F につづいて Jap、Sp は 2 位で、4 位 It、5 位 L となっている。

2) 222 の Jap 借入語を調べてみると (1994) 飲食、芸術、仕事、貨幣などに関する名詞が圧倒的である。

時として Jap [a] > E [ɔ]（[æ]）(basho)、Jap [l] > E [r] (bira) のような音置換も見られる。

3) 例　（数字：OED 初出年）

ama(1954)　dashi(1963)　itai-itai(1969)　karate(1955)　kata (型)(1954)　kogai(1970)　kokeshi(1959)　Mikimoto(1956)　mingei(1960)　oshibori(1959)　oyama(1963)　pachinko(1953)　rumaki(春巻き)(1965)　shabu-shabu(1970)　shiatsu(1967)　shi-

shi(1970)　shokku(1971)　sumotori(1973)　Suntory(1959)
tamari(しょうゆ)(1977)　teppanyaki(1970)　teriyaki(1962)
yakuza(1964)　yokozuna(1966)　zaikai(1968)
bento　yakitori　enka　oseibo　karaoke　hanamichi　daruma
sushi　ofuro　origami　Noh　sumi-e　gaijin　endaka　keire-
tsu(系列)(1991)　karoshi(過労死)(1990-)　three K's salary-
man(1988-)　karate　ninja　walkman　Honda(〜Accord)
Mazda　habatsu　ken(県)

⑦　翻訳借入

時折原語を翻訳して借入する。

F　third age / flea-market / black comedy(＜comédie noire)
Ch　barefoot doctor
G　metric space / round trip
Jap　bullet train

　　フランス語のように借入を歓迎しない言語ではしばしば翻訳借入による。複合力に欠けるので複合語の借入は句で表すことが多い。

14.3　造語

借入によらず自前の wordstock を用いて新語をつくる(⇒複合)。

(1) 宇宙科学、科学の進歩に伴う

　　capsule　spaceman　platform　station　automation
　　e-mail(1994-)　internetter(1993-)　hacker　password　modern
　　mouse　software　floppy disc　aerobics　eye/blood bank

(2) 新製品など

　　jeans(＜Gene[＝Genoa] cloth)〜panti-hose(1963)

(3) perestroika[＝radical change (in economic policy)](1989-)
　　thirdwave[＝younger generation of human feminists](1992-)

Kleenex < clean(K- は Kodak のまね。英語は k で始まる語が少ないので選ばれた)

Xerox < Gk　xero [＝dry]

（4）隠語(argot)

pal < Romany　ph(v)al [＝brother]

kinchin [＝young] < G　kindchen

（5）俗語から

rad < radical [＝excellent]

abfab < absolutely fabulous

14.4 転換

(1)① 最近の語彙形成の傾向は(1989 年の数字による)

複合	29.5% ⎫ 53.7%
派生	24.2% ⎭
転換	19.6% ⎫ 37.7%
短化(逆形成、blend などを含む)	18.1% ⎭
借入	7.5%

　上の数字でみるように、転換(接辞なしで新しい品詞をつくる)による語彙形成は PE の特徴の 1 つで、とくに口語できわめてひんぱんである。verb＋particle ＞ N が 19 c 以後ひんぱんとなる(play-off, check-up)。

② 20 c に入ってからの転換を調べてみると

1)A ＞ N がもっとも多く、つづいて 2)N ＞ V, 3)V ＞ N, 4)N ＞ A の順である。その他(A ＞ V, V ＞ A, Adv ＞ A)は少ない。

(2)① A ＞ N

poor / heavy / (you're my) crazy / disposables / (a) nasty / short / forget a slight / lose one's cool / (five) possibles / (a) natural / intellectual / an Olympic *hopeful* / keep one's *cool* / suspect(Aとしては18c初め、Nとしては17c初めから廃れかけたが、19c初めFの影響で生き残った) / in quiet / *sufficient* of his friends / several / various / cf.　a great many

an exhibit was related to war *dead*　　　(Cornwell *Potter's* 204)
she's one of the *greats*　　　　　　　　　　(Robbins *Love* 246)

② N > A
名詞の前位置を占める名詞に形容詞の働きをさせるのはきわめてふつうの派生である。しかし、choice, chief のように比較級(最上級)をもったり、standard のように叙述的に用いられたりするものもある。

(the) *majority* (*minority*) agreement / (a) *chain* coffee drinker / *chance* encounters / (an) *idiot* child / (the) *head* (bookkeeper) / (a) *standard* view > …is *standard* / *miniature* camera / choicest / chiefest

Mary's voice was *steel*　　　　　　　(Sheldon *Windmills* 386)
　　cf. Every single piece of equipment was *state of the art*
　　　　　　　　　　　　　　　　　　　(Sheldon *Windmills* 19)

③　N > V (= denominative verb)
幼児はV > N よりも早く習得する。独立動詞があってもしばしば作られることが多いので、例えば、gift を動詞に使うことについてかなり多くの人が反対している(1975年のAEではYes　5%―No 95%)。また author のように名詞に強く結びつけられているものの動詞化にもまだ強い反対がある(1975年のAEではYes　10%―No 90%)。

anger / access (files) / breakfast / bed (with) / bottle / chair / corner / conquest / diet / fax him a message / father / fault / host [最近] / holiday / inch / impact /

other girls were *waitressing* / He *mouths* the word 'mother' / pleasure[= please] / parent(最近) / rendezvoused with / rubbish[= criticize] / research / service[= repair] / star / shylock / Three enemy planes were *sighted* / fault / vacation / We'll *party* all night / handbag(Thatcher 元英国首相に連想され「男を支配し、おしつける」) / concorde to America(< Concorde) / exit

I *receipted* them [= bullets] to him.　　　(Cornwell *All* 127)

④　V > N

　「感覚、精神的、物理的行為」を示す動詞からの派生名詞で単音節であることが原則である。また口語の特徴でもある。give がもっともふつうで、これに have, take, さらに make, get がつづく。N は前に a(まれに複数形、the)をとる。

　give は名詞の前に形容詞がつくのが圧倒的だが、have / take は逆につかないことのほうが多い。

　また、give / take では 3 人称主語が、have は 1、2 人称主語が多い。

1) buy / bath / bathe / cry / catch(es) / dash / dive / (get) a feel / grunt / guess / (have) a go [= try] / (get) the hang / (give) laugh(s) / (give) look (of contempt) / arrange a meet / move / thank you for the *invite* / beyond *compare* / offer / peep / ride / rest / it is an easy *read* / it is a more interesting *read* / scare / start / spread / shudder / swim / smoke / stroll / (have a good) try / take / tug / (have a hard) think / turn / (have a quick) wash / have a worry / wish / walk / win

Another *wait*　　　　　　　　　　　(Archer *Prod* 252)
The *wait* is anguish for them　　　　　(Cornwell *All* 165)

You're not doing *the rewrite* (Robbins *Storyteller* 162)

2) be closing in for the *kill*(えものに迫る) / long time no see / How long a *wait* will there be for a table / his *find* is〜a new *find* / healthy *eats*[= food] / edit[= editing] / shop[= shopping] / affect / here is a *surprise* / the *commute* is too long / strengthen their *resolve*

cf. give this remark a good *thinking* over

(Klavan *Crime* 193)

⑤ A > V

secret / best(やっつける) / empty / calm / ready (him for sleep) / wet (one's lips) / brief

⑥ Adv > N

You hire detectives on a *maybe*(不確かな事柄)(Koontz *Face* 79)

14.5 派生(derivation)

　PE の語彙形成力は複合につぎ生産的である。接辞の中には派生力があって、外来語などが入って来ると添加されうるもの(productive なもの)——例えば -ness / -ism / -er / -ize / -wise など——と、新しい形にはもはや添加されず、決まったいい方にのみ見られるもの(unproductive なもの)——例えば -th / -dom など——と2つがある。

　すでに同じ意味をもった項目があると接辞によって新しい形をつくることがしばしば拒否される(blocking)。

　　thief があるので *stealer

　　bad があるので *ungood

　　graciousness があるので *graciosity

同じ名詞派生接辞でも基体の素性に反応するものがある。例えば -ness は本来起源語(cf. kindness)、最近は外来起源語にもつくが、-ity は外来語に

つくのが原則である。

  curiosity   — curiousness
  suitability   — suitableness
 *graciosity   — graciousness
  sobriety   — soberness
  normality   — normalness
         quietness — quietude

どの言語でも、接尾辞を接頭辞より好む。3対1の割合である。V-final言語では5対1、V-medial言語(SVO, OVS)では2対1、V-initial言語では1対1の割合である。

14.5.1 接辞
14.5.1.1 接尾辞(suffix)

多くの言語同様、英語も接頭辞に比べて2倍もの種類があり、生産的なものが多い。199の接尾辞のうち、135は名詞を形成するもの、52は形容詞を形成するもの、12は動詞を形成するものである。もっともひんぱんな名詞から形容詞を形成する接尾辞は、-y, -al, -ful, -ous, -less, -ly, -ic, -ish である。
（1）名詞を形成する接尾辞
 ① -ness
  上でものべたように基体の種類をとわず、形容詞について名詞をつくる。最近は既存の illness に対して wellness が使われ始める。非常に生産的であるが、?bigness, ?beautifulness。
  togetherness / outgoingness / black and blue*ness*
 ② -ist, -er
  すでに12cから baptist, evangelist、17cには linguist, imperialist, chemist, violinist のように生産を始めていたが、19c scientist から反対論議が始まり、しばらく使われなかった。しかし今世紀に入って生産的となる。[t, n]で終る動詞以外のもの、-al, -ion のあとにつき

やすい。-ist は「人」、-er は「人」、「機械」を表す。

evolutionist, feminist, dramatist, tobacconist, copyist (cf. copier), typist (cf. typewriter), dartist, panelist—*paneller

③ -ess

最近 sexism のため(⇒16章 性差)だんだん使われなくなってきている。

stewardess, actress, heiress, (a charming) hostess, millionairess, ただし murderess はよく使われる。

④ -ese

journalese, motherese, Americanese, headlinese, officialese

⑤ -ee

受身の意味を表す。

interviewee, divorcee, biographee, evacuee, selectee, addressee, payee, holdupee

⑥ -dom

snobdom, stardom

⑦ -ette

maisonette

⑧ -ism

ableism, weightism, feminism, ageism

(2) 形容詞を形成する接尾辞

① -ish

N について	foolish
A について	coldish, tallish, shortish
時について	2:30 ish, fiftyish, dinnerish

② -able

原則的には他動詞につくが、まれに自動詞にもつく。受身の意味を表すことが多い。

lovable, burnable, (machine)washable, fanable(star), unkillable, agreeable, perishable, knowlegeable, companionabl(y)

how attractive and personable she was　　　(Hailey *Hotel* 42)

③ -y

tony, peachy, comfy

④ -en

[d, ʃ, k, s, z] に終る N につきやすく、最近は「メタフォリック」な意味で用いられやすい。

golden (hour) (cf. gold watch), leaden (cf. lead pipe), しかし the *golden* cross (Sheldon *Sands* 78), oaken, silken (ease) (cf. silk pyjamas), waxen, brazen (imprudence), ashen, woollen sheets, wooden chair

（3） 動詞を形成する接尾辞

① -en

非生産的。A、N について。

deepen, moisten, hearten, lengthen

② -ize

urbanize

（4） 副詞を形成する接尾辞

① -wise

1940 年ごろから N について「に関して」の意味で最近よく使われる。最初 AE で、のち BE へも。

Weatherwise, (we can't complain).

businesswise, moneywise, taxwise, clotheswise, healthwise, fitnesswise, saleswise, successwise, etiquettewise, drinkingwise

② -ly

(buy, use one's funds) greenly

(say it) matter-of-factly　　　(Sheldon *Bloodline* 316)

③ -ward

I drove officeward (Sanders *Luck* 42)

14.5.1.2 接頭辞(prefix)

とくに un-, non-, de-, ex-, re- などが生産的である。

① non-, un-

non- は OED 補遺版では 500 以上(Webster では 3000 以上)の N, A につく。un- は A, Adv、ときに N, V にもつく。

nonaction(1968), nonbook(1960s),

nonevent(1967), nonsystem(1972),

nonworker(1967), nonending(1969), nonliving(1972)

unseen―*unsee, unspoken―*unspeak,

unhappy, unsure, unclear,

*untall, *unbusy, *unround,

unpublicity, unfreedom,

unman(V), unbook(V), unreplace (him), unchoose,

unbeknown to〜,

unpoor[= not very rich but not so poor],

uncouth

② re-

最近「再使用の」意味で使われる。自動詞につくときは他動詞となるが例外もある。「状態」「行為」にふつうつかない。

reprocess(spent fuel), recycle(bottles), regarbage(plastics)

relive (the past), rethink,

(You never) remarried (Sheldon *Rage* 172)

she'd be remarried (Steel *Ghost* 218)

reinvent, regroup, retake one's seat, rekiss, rebecome(以上 SOD),

reappear

③ ir-

　irregardless (irrespective のまねで反対も多い)

④ de-

　deregulate, deinternationalize, declassify, deactivated, deselection, deskill, deair, decelerate

⑤ dis-

　disinformation [= deliberately false information especially as supplied by one government to another or to the public]
　in disrepair (傷んだ状態)
　disremember [= forget]　　　　　　　　(Sanders *Pleasures* 335)

⑥ mid-, under-

　Her dream has just blown up *mid-flight* (= Adv)

　　　　　　　　　　　　　　　　　　　(Cornwell *Body* 164)

　over- に対して underwhelming　　　　　(Sanders *Risk* 290)

14.5.2　結合形 (combining form)

接頭辞よりも PE では生産的である。

① 接頭辞的結合形

arch-	archconservative
bio-	biogas, biosphere, bioengineering
eco-	ecosystem, ecoclimate, ecosphere
micro-	microchip, microfloppy, microwave
immuno-	immunochemistry, immunosuppression
anti-	antidepression, antinuclear, antihero
counter-	countereffect, counterintuitive
semi-	semioccasionally (AE) [= sometimes]
ethno-	ethno-law

hyper-	hyperfine
mega-	megagame
mini-	(1966年以降) minicar, miniskirt, minisuccess, minicomputer, miniwar
stereo-	stereophonic, stereoscopic
super-	over- は望ましくない意味だがこれは「賛美」を意味する。
	superfine, supermarket, supersonic, super-special

② 接尾辞的結合形

-scape	seascape, moonscape, soundscape, streetscape
-ster	(一時死んでいたが悪い意味で20cに復活) popster, pollster, roadster, speedster
-gate	koreagate cf. Watergate
-nik	beatnik, sputnik
-proof	burglar-proof, fool-proof
-speak	computerspeak, winespeak cf. Orwell's newspeak
-happy	(1940〜) gadget-happy, travel-happy
-drome	sportsdrome, syndrome
-genic	photogenic, videogenic
-tron / -tronic(s)	autotronic, electronics
-burger	beefburger, baconburger
-wise	career-wise, you're in good shape right now (Hailey *Detective* 583) cf. 14.5.1.1 (4)「副詞を形成する接尾辞」 he was not as *streetwise* (A) as I

(Sanders *Trial* 176)

14.6 逆形成 (back formation)

19c 以降非常に生産的となっていく。N > V が多い。最近増える傾向にある。OED 補遺版によると 1924 年 1 個、1933-38 年では 2 個だったのが 1958-59 年では 5 個、1960-71 年では 23 個になる。

difficult は名詞 difficulty からの逆形成であることはほとんどわからないほどとけ込んでいる。

もっともふつうの過程は名詞(とくに複合語)から動詞を作るものである。接尾辞削除がふつうで illicit > licit (19c) のような接頭辞削除によるものは少ない。

逆形成は制約をうけることがある。housekeep, speedread などは、すべての時制、人称に使えるとは限らない。

 *he housekept / *he speedreads

① enthuse < enthusiasm / intuit < intuition / orientate < orientation / mass-produce(1940) < mass-production / self-destruct < self-destruction （destruct はないのに）/ burgle < burglar / air-condition < airconditioner / book-keep < book-keeper / house-keep < house-keeper / tape-record < tape-recorder / scuba dive < scuba diver / sightsee < sightseeing / proofread < proof-reading / windowshop < windowshopping / self-adjust < self-adjustment / name-drop(1960) < name-dropping / automate (1954) < automation

② lazy > laze(V) / peevish > peeve(N, V)(1952) / complicity > complicit(A) / raunchy > raunch(N)

③ unflappable > flappable

14.7 複合 (compounding)

(1)　英語はドイツ語と同じく複合を得意とする。フランス語は不得意 (top modèle, baby-star) で、複合語のもつ機能を統語関係で示す。

　　現在の語形成のうちではもっともふつうで、その内訳は多いものからあげると複合名詞 (26.2%) (N 2つから成るものが多い。ついで1つは A)、複合形容詞 (21%)、複合動詞 (1%) (一方が N または Particle)、その他 (0.2%) の順となる。

　　構成をみると、英語の複合語は圧倒的に透明 (endocentric) 型で不透明な (exocentric) 型は少ない。その比はおおよそ 88%：12% である。名詞複合、動詞複合は前者のタイプ、形容詞複合、副詞複合は後者のタイプの頻度が高い。

　　英語の複合語は右側 (第2) 要素が全体の意味や品詞を決めることが多い (head-final)。

cat*house* [= a type of a house] (cf. a house cat)

$[[\text{baby}]_N - [\textit{sit}]_V]_V$

Welsh などは逆に左側に主要部が来る (head-initial)。

jwg laeth [= jug milk] (ミルクを入れる容器)。

(2)　派生/屈折形態論があまりない言語は複合をよく利用する。ここでは2つの単語が並ぶ句から複合へは簡単にいきつく。

　　派生を多用する言語は複合を全く使わないか、少しですませられる。

(3)　複合はつねに語彙化 (lexicalize) されるとは限らない。もし語の連鎖が複合として語彙化されたら話手の語彙はとてつもなく大きいものとなろう。しばしば複合として定着しない一時的な語の連鎖が起こる。英語では4語から成る複合はほとんどない。

hunger strike / alibi witness / 'motor-voter' denial / 5-key direct access disc selection / hi fi 5-disc CD changer

（4）複合は´＿＿が原則である。ただし＿＿´(apple pie, blood red)もある。

（5）複合は統語的に分離されない(ただし等位構造のときは例外。voter anger *and* outrage)。決定詞、所有格、形容詞などを中に入れない。
*black *brown* bird

（6）複合の要素は屈折形を欠く。
*dark*er*room ＜ darkroom

（7）複合語の種類

（ⅰ）語根複合語(root compound)
N, A, V, P など単純語からなる複合語。例えば hunger strike, sea sick, blackboard, aftercare など。

（ⅱ）総合的複合語(synthetic compound)
主要部(第2要素)が動詞から派生されている(deverbal)もの。例えば CD changer, disc selection, dressmaking など。

14.7.1 名詞複合語

非常に多い。N_iN_j のとき N_i が複数の場合は例外的(cf. communications gap)。

① NN： boyfriend bell-boy
   VN： turntable
   NV： busstop chickenfeed
   VV： make-believe pass-fail
   VAdv： get-together (a) comeback
   AN： fast-food greencard

② P(Particle)N：　　　off-(off)-Broadway after-effect
　　　　　　　　　　　in-group in-car
   P(Particle)V：　　　input overkill

第14章 語彙　125

　　　　VP(Particle)：(多い)　teach-in / hold-up / drop-in / black-out / sit-in / follow-up / checkup / break-through / lead-in / handout / frame-up / lie-in fly-in / (a) holding back
③　　[NN] N：air cushion belt / kitchen towel rack / job opportunity discrimination

14.7.2　形容詞複合語

①　NA：　　　　　top heavy / streetwise(-smart) / trouble-free / razor-thin(1971)
　　[AN](ed)：　　double date / bright-eyed
　　　　　　　　　(the government is so *red-tape* that…(FEN))
　　VAdv：　　　　drop-dead (blonde) / get-well card
　　NV(ptp)：　　 airborne / moon-struck / cockroach-infested *Harvard-trained* pathologist
　　　　　　　　　　　　　　　　　　　　(Cornwell *Unnatural* 355)
　　　　　　　　　store-bought sandwiches　　(Hailey *Detective* 187)
　　　　　　　　　be *chair-destined*(電気椅子にかけられる)
　　　　　　　　　　　　　　　　　　　　(Hailey *Detective* 509)
　　AA：　　　　　icy-cold
　　AV(prp)：　　 good-looking / easy-going
　　AV(ptp)：　　 soft-spoken / deep-set
　　AdvV(ptp)：　 well-read / hard-boiled(1927～)
　　NN(ed)：　　　world class (pianist) / (be) jet-lagged / time tested (be) marriage-*minded*　　(Hailey *Wheels* 190)
②　P(Particle)N：in-depth / off-beat
　　P(Particle)A：oversensitive

P(Particle)V(ptp)： underprivileged
P(Particle)A： off-white
VP(Particle)： see-through / put-down / walk-up （apartment） / a lived-in room

14.7.3　動詞複合語

① NV：(多い)　gatecrash / videorecord / sightsee(Rome) / gift-wrap(this) / hand-select (your team) / spoon-feed
AV：　fine-tune / sweet-talk / glad-hand
AN：　bad-mouth / blue-pencil
NN：(多い)　data-bank / handbag / honeymoon / skyjack / mickey-mouse / skyrocket
　　　jump-start his heart with a third cup of coffee
　　　　　　　　　　　　　（Dunning *Booked* 337）
VA：　tail-safe / blow-dry (one's hair)
VV：　test-drive
VN：　singsong　　　　　　　（Robbins *Storyteller* 77）
AdvV：　half-expect (hope) / backdate / double-cross
IntInt：　pooh-pooh
② P(Particle)V： overpower / undercharacterize
　　　　download(vi)　　　（Cornwell *Unnatural* 38）
　　　　out-bluff
VP(Particle)： count-down

最近カナダ英語では to fund raise / to problem solve のような複合動詞がひんぱんになりつつある。babysit を除くことのところ複合動詞がほとんどなかったためかもしれない(Marie-Lucie Tarpent (1998) "Changes in English." *Liguist List* 9-668-1 (May 7. 1998))。

14.7.4 その他

① e-mail (V)
   ad-lib (V) (< ad-libitum [= according to pleasure])
② 文、節、句、相当内容を複合語とする
   an off-the-record comment / a once-in-a-lifetime experience / on-the-job training / a man-bites-dog story / his not-so-white shirt
③ 切離構造 (tmesis)（口語で）
   hoo-*bloody*-ray
   im-*bloody*-possible

14.8 短化 (abbreviation)

　短化は短化されたものを文字の連続として発音される。語を省略する歴史は古く、and を &、generale を gle のように表すことが 15 c 以前から行われていた。1855 年には初めて縮約辞典 (Courtenay 1885) が出た。1950 年以後 Webster をみるとわかるように約 55 万の収録語の 1% にも及ぶ。

　今日、その便利さのゆえに、化学、生物学、コンピューター、教育、運輸、軍隊などいろいろな局面で使われている。

　アクロニムもそうであるが、短化の出力も最初専門語であっても一般化されることが多い。アクロニムは完全形が十分確立されないうちにつくられるのに対して、短化はもとの形が十分確立してから起こる。

① technical > tech / rehabilitation > rehab / hyperactive > hyper / glamorous > glam / fabulous > fab / psychoanalyze > psycho / vegetables > veggies / cigarette > ciggy
② situation comedy > sitcom / show business > show biz / night gown > nightie / goal keeper > goalie / popular singer > pop-

singer / high fidelity > hi-fi

Adidas trainers > Adidas / Danish pastry > Danish / microwave oven > microwave / life sentence > (he got) life brother > bro

③ advantage > van / accompany > comp / contraconceptive pill > pill

④ undergraduate > undergrad

⑤ ex-wife, ex-husband > ex

cf. her ex lives here

14.9 アクロニム(acronym)

略字を語として発音する。短化よりもまれ(ある数字によればアクロニムの 29%に対して短化は 46%)。多くは固有名詞、組織名、委員会名、商標、コンピューター、宇宙科学、化学などで使われ、3〜9文字から成る。

```
DOS    <  disk-operating system
Rom    <  read only memory
RAM    <  random-access memory
CAD    <  computer-aided design
Coke   <  cocacola
AIDS   <  acquired immune deficiency syndrome
DJ     <  disc jockey
DIY    <  do it yourself
MIT    <  Massachusetts Institute of Technology
UFO    <  unidentified flying object
TESL   <  teaching English as a second language
```

14.10　混成(portmanteau)

　Lewis Carroll に発する。19 c 半ばまではまれだが、20 c 後半から雑誌、新聞などで商用、ファッション、スポーツ、旅行、エンターテイメント、科学、技術、政治、家庭にかかわる名前に簡潔で、意表をつく便利な方法として愛用されている。

　2つの要素A，Bがあるとき、（ⅰ）Aの第1音とBの最後の音（billion＋millionaire ＞ billionaire）、（ⅱ）AまたはBをそのまま含む（sound＋sensational ＞ soundsational）、（ⅲ）AまたはBと一方の中央音節を含む（copy＋electronic ＞ copytron）。なおこの混成はフランス語にも入る。

　　faction ＜ fact＋fiction / skyjack ＜ sky＋hijack / guesstimate ＜ guess＋estimate / stagflation ＜ stagnation＋inflation / Chunnel ＜ Channel＋tunnel / heliport ＜ helicopter＋airport / breathalyser ＜ breath＋analyser / dresshirt ＜ dress＋shirt / Euro-vision ＜ European＋vision / xerocopy ＜ xerox＋copy / blaxploitation ＜ blacks＋exploitation / skuit (1990s) ＜ skirt＋suit

14.11　語彙の意味

　語の元来の意味が新しい意味に取って代られることはまれだが、新しい意味が付け加えられることがよくある。動詞、形容詞、副詞（全体の3分の1）より名詞に圧倒的に多い（全体の3分の2）。

　現代の傾向としては、付け加えられた意味は口語、俗語、卑語的なレベルで使われる。

　　snow 'heroin' / waste 'kill' / boy 'toilet' / fiddle 'chest' / redundant 'out of work'

意味変化は特殊な意味よりも一般的な意味を、悪い意味よりも良い意味を、具体的な意味よりも抽象的な意味を発達させる傾向がある。

第 15 章　発音

15.1　概論

　ことばはつねにじっさいの文脈において使われている文体、使用者の社会的背景、さらに特定の音の語中、音節中で占める位置、強勢の有無、文アクセント、休止といった要因にたえずさらされ、音は「揺れ」ている。これは変化への準備、予備軍である。

（1）同化
　　statement ＞ [steɪpmənt]
　　this year ＞ [ðɪʃjɪə]

（2）脱落
　① last year ＞ [lɑːsjɪə]　　　aspects ＞ [æspeks]
　　 rapidly ＞ [ræpɪli]　　　 of course ＞ [əkɔːs]
　　 also ＞ [ɔsəʊ]　　　　　can't remember ＞ [kɑːntɪmembə]
　　 asked him ＞ [ɑːstɪm]
　② interest ＞ [ɪntrəst]　　　similar ＞ [sɪmlə]
　　 library ＞ [laɪbri]　　　　perhaps ＞ [pæps]
　　 actually ＞ [ækʃli]　　　　going to be ＞ [gənəbi]
　③ satisfied ＞ [sæssfaɪd]　　we've been ＞ [wivβin]

cared for > [keːdfə]

BE： 18 c 前半から始まった V の変化(ō, ē の 2 重母音化、æ〜ā、ɒ〜ɔː、ɔə > ɔː、r > φ など)は 19 c 中にだんだん固まっていき、20 c はじめには大体 PE の音段階に達する。

AE： BE よりも変化少なく(ō, ē の 2 重母音化、æ〜ɑ:〜ɔː など)安定。

15.2 / C /

(1) 「声」のゆれ

① [s]〜[z] / [θ]〜[ð] / [f]〜[v] / [tʃ]〜[dʒ]

	AE	BE
greasy		s〜z
resource		zɔː〜s (50%〜45%)
chrysanthemum		sæ〜zæ (61%〜39%)
venison		s ([z] まれ)
Mrs	zɪz〜sɪz	sɪz
baths		ðz〜θs (50%〜50%)
nephew	———	f〜v (79%〜21%)
Greenwich	———	tʃ〜dʒ
sandwich	———	dʒ〜tʃ (54%〜47%)
with	θ	ð
	([ð] は NYC、Northwest など)	
houses	zɪz〜sɪz, zɪs, sɪs (最近広い地域で s 形も聞かれる)	
absolve		z〜s (z の方が優勢)

② partner > pardner (V__n でも ʃ)

shut up > shaddup　　　　　　　　　(Hailey *Wheels* 429)

（2）削除

① [t, d, n] が速い speech の語末で。

old men　　fifteen miles

$$\begin{bmatrix} +\text{voiced} \\ C \end{bmatrix}\begin{bmatrix} +\text{voiced} \\ C \end{bmatrix} \text{あるいは} \begin{bmatrix} -\text{voiced} \\ C \end{bmatrix}\begin{bmatrix} -\text{voiced} \\ C \end{bmatrix} \quad (\text{find, act})$$
$$\qquad\qquad\downarrow\qquad\qquad\qquad\qquad\qquad\downarrow$$
$$\qquad\qquad\phi\qquad\qquad\qquad\qquad\qquad\phi$$

② C＿C, ＿CC の文脈で C が落ちる。

sof(t)ness（口語）

months > ns　　　　twelfth > lθ

pants > ns　　　　 acts > ks

eighth > θ　　　　 clothes > z

zð > z

　is/was/has/does＋the/there

　Is the radio on? > ɪzə…

③ l > φ　　falcon salt told（以上 EstE でこの 25 年以来）

④ r > φ

無強勢音節にあって [r] と隣接する [r]。しかし最近 BE では隣接しないときでも落ちることがある。

library > laɪbəri

February > febjuəri

temporary > tempəri

temperature > tempətʃə

⑤ n > φ

goverNment

⑥ h > φ

1) 無強勢音節で。機能語の語頭で。

histŏric > ɪ
hystéria > ɪ
has, have, he, him, her
ve[h]ícular〜vé[h]icle
pro[h]íbit〜pro[h]ibítion

2)   AE BE
 human hju: hju:
 humor ([ju:]は後退しており NYC, Philadelphia など
      で聞かれる)

⑦ j > φ
 1) 唇音(labial), 軟口蓋音(velar)の後では保たれる (beauty/cute)
 2) [θ ð], [t d s z n] など舌頂音(coronal)C のあとでは
  ⅰ) AE では j→φ
  ⅱ) BE では j を保つ。しかし若い人たちは j→φ を強めている
  ⅲ) AustE では ⅰ)と ⅱ)の中間

	AE	BE	AustE
blue	φ	φ	φ
cute	j	j	j
new	φ	j〜φ(若い人)	j
lewd	φ	j〜φ	φ〜j

(3) 挿入
 ① 挿入音が第1音と場所に関して、第2音と声に関して一致する。
  φ>t / n, l__s (sense > sents prince > nts)
       (else)
  φ>p / m__θ (warmpth)
  φ>k / ŋ__θ (length strength)
  φ>k   (BE, Australasian 方言で)-ing のあとで [k]
       nothing [-ɪŋk]

$\phi > t$ / s, f__## (once*t*, cliff*t*) (AE 方言)　　(##は語境界を示す)

② 侵入的 r (BE)

今日しばしば RP で。connected speech の現象。最初 [ə] のあとで挿入されたのが他の母音にも拡大する。

$\phi > r$ / ə, ɔː, ɑː, əː__##V (V = ə)

they saw(r)a young lady / no idea(r)of it /

China(r)and Japan / law(r)and order / drama(r)and music

(4) 母音化

①

$l > ɫ$ / $\left\{ \begin{array}{l} -\left\{ \begin{array}{l} C \\ \# \end{array} \right\} \\ V\_V \end{array} \right\}$　(milk full fill)

　　　　　　　(jelly [dʒeɫi])　　　　(#は語中境界を示す)

この変化は RP にも入って来ており、間もなく標準化される (Wells 1982：§3.4.4)。

② j > i

　　　　　1949　　　1988

　piano　pjǽnoʊ　>　piǽnəʊ

(5) 声門閉鎖音化(glottalization)

① BE の特徴の1つで、[p t k tʃ] を [ʔ] (glottal stop)で置換する。

1)音節末(syllable-final)の位置で

2)V, L, N が先行している位置で(happy/teacher [tíːʔtʃə])

語末の [ʔ] はいずれ消失すると思われる(中国語ではすでに消失)(Aitchison 1991:126-7)。

② t > ʔ

Australasian E　butter [t] > [ʔ]

(6) r を発音する(rhotic)

AE では rhotic が prestige のしるしとして NY を含めた地域で拡大

しつつある。RP は原則は nonrhotic だが、EstE や若い人の中には rhotic の傾向が見られる。

    center, part

    注　rhotic に意識的でありすぎて φ→r が起こることがある。

      pawn > pɔrn

（7）音交替
- ① ʒ～dʒ　　garage
- ② ʃ～sk　　schedule(BE では原則 [ʃ]、AE では原則 [sk])
- ③ w～hw < wh >

	AE	BE
where, when…	w(圧倒的) (NYC, Boston など ではかつての prestige form [hw] も)	w～hw

15.3　/V/

一般傾向としては
- ① 2重母音 > 長母音 > 短母音(＝低母音 > 高母音)の順で変化しやすい。
- ② 強勢のない母音はあるものよりも変化を受けやすい。
- ③ 長母音は上げを好み、短母音は上げ/下げいずれも好む。

今日起こりつつある変化は(ⅰ)持続変化、(ⅱ)水平変化、(ⅲ)2重母音化/単音化。垂直変化は AE にみられるが比較的まれ。

（1）持続変化(短/長化)
- ① 短化
  - 1) BE で ɔː > ɒ /＿＿[f θ s]
  -                   / [s f]＿＿l

soft, coffee, off, often, soften, cough, cloth, broth, froth, moth, cross, loss, salt (ɔ: 43% − ɒ 57%), falter

2) BE で u: > ʊ/＿＿[m n]

room ([u:] 82%-[ʊ] 19%) (AE でも [u:]。ただし [ʊ〜ʌ] も、Hawaii, North California などで), boom, boon, moon, noon, soon, spoon

3) u: > ʊ / ＿＿[d f k s t]

BE: rood [u:], roost [u:], root [u:], roof [u:〜ʊ], rook [ʊ]
AE: hoof [ʊ] がふつう。[u:] は Central Pennsylvania, Virginia などで。[ʌ] も増えつつある。roof [u:] が圧倒的。[ʊ] は Midwest, Northwest などで。root [u:] が圧倒的。[ʊ] は Midwest, Chicago などで。

　Canadian English で最近。一説では California の 10 代の女性の発音から拡大 (food)。かつては Ulster, Mid & SW Scot, England の Midlands, Norfolk, AE の South などで。今日では universal になりつつある。

4) i: > ɪ　breeches (BE)

② 長化

1) æ > æ: / ＿＿[b d g dʒ z m n]

単音節語で。BE では [æə] のように 2 重母音化する教育のある形が聞かれる。

　AE でも Philadelphia では [eːə]、NY では [iːə] と上げられた 2 重母音が聞かれる。

dab, glad, bag, badge, jazz, jam, man

2) ʊ > u: / ＿＿m (BE)

	1949	1988
broom	ʊ(〜u:)	u:(〜ʊ)

3) 無強勢音節の語末/音節末で

ɪ > i: / ___ $\begin{Bmatrix} \$ \\ \#\# \end{Bmatrix}$

($は音節境界を示す)

AEではすでに広くいきわたっているが、BEでも若い人たちの間で広がり始めた。

money, happy, city, beauty, country

AEでは processes も [i:z] と発音されることが多い。

(2) 水平変化(前舌/後舌)

① 前舌化

1) a > æ / ___ ʊ (AE)

account, count, down

2) ɑ: > æ: (BE)

lather, chaff, pastoral, Glasgow

3) ɑ: > æ < a > (BE)

短化を伴う前舌化。AE の影響も考えられる。

drastic	æ(88%);	AE—ɑ: (12%)
exasperate	æ(54%);	AE—ɑ: (46%)
plastic	æ(92%);	AE—ɑ: (8%)
substantial	æ(93%);	AE—ɑ: (7%)
lather	æ(28%);	AE—ɑ: (72%)
pastoral	æ～ɑ:	

3)′ (London English) ɒʊ～ʌʊ

ɒʊ は同一音節内の [l] の前で保たれるが、その他では [ʌʊ]。

roll [rɒʊl], old, cold // load [lʌʊd]

4) ʌ > æ (BE)

cut, jump

5) ɒ: > ɑ: (AE)(第2音として)

bought ɒ:～ɑ: autumn, talk

5)′ ɔ: > ɑ: (AE)

20c 初めに Western Pennsylvania, Eastern New England などで始まったが今日ではあらゆるところに拡大し、New England の東部、Pittsburg、さらに Canada でも定着。ただし、New England の南、Great Lake 地域では区別されている。

walk : dock,　　caught : dot

② 後舌化

1) æ: > ɑ:

transfer, translate

2) フォルマントのちがいに基づく前舌/後舌化の検証

	1962 (F_2-F_1)	1982 (F_2-F_1)
ʌ > æ	514	555 (come)
uː > ʉ	630	802 (food)
æ > ɑː	998	902 (mad)

ʌ > ɔ (EstE) (done, government, some, worry)

(3) 垂直変化(上げ/下げ)

① 上げ

1) æ－上げ (AE とくに北部 America で) / __C(C)##

æ が [ɛ] へ上げられ2重母音化 [ɛə] する。単音節語に多くみられる。文脈はしばしば割れ (breaking) のそれと重複する。

C = [b d g dʒ f v θ s z ʃ m n]

half, man, past, bag

2) æ > e (AE)

Northwest, Great Lakes などで [e]

South, New England, Pennsylvania などで [e]〜[æ]

NY－Washington 回廊、Northern California などで [æ]

3) ə > ɪ (AE の Upper & Low South)

soda

4) aʊ > oʊ (AE 北部方言)

out

　　cf. Canadian Raising：カナダ英語で例えばwife[wʌɪf]〜wives[waɪv], house[ʌʊs]〜houses[aʊz]となる過程。

② 下げ

　1) ʊ(> ɣ > ʌ > ɒ) > ɑ (SouthernE, Scot, AEの方言など)
　　cup, luck
　2) e > æ とくにCanadianEで最近起こり始めた。最初有声閉鎖音の前で。さらに無声閉鎖音の前でもときに起こる。
　　egg, beg / beck

(4) 2重母音化/単音化

① 2重母音化

　1) 割れ－[ɪ]/[ʊ]の挿入 (AE)
　　æ > æɪ　前方摩擦音・軟口蓋音の前で (grass, half, bag, hang)
　　e > eɪ　後部歯茎音・軟口蓋音の前で (measure, pleasure, egg, peg)
　　o > oʊ　軟口蓋音の前で (fog)
　　C = [f θ s v ʃ g]
　　BEでも＿lの文脈でi → iə (feel [fiːəl])
　　まれにtrash, cash > æɪ

　2) [l]の母音化による
　　l > ɫ > ʊ
　　solve, involve, resolve, absolve, dissolve, evolve, golf

　3) $\begin{Bmatrix} iː > ɪi \\ uː > ʊu \end{Bmatrix}$ / ＿(C)##
　　第1要素は第2要素よりも、より開き中舌的。
　　sea, see, tea, seat, feed
　　shoe, do, bamboo, tooth, school

　3)′ iː > eɪ (AE Appalachia, Tennessee, Kentucky)

people

BE でも deity, spontaneity

3)″i: > əɪ (AustE)

eat

4) uː > ɪu (AE とくに Midwest (Michigan, Wisconsin, Minesota など))

5) æ > eːə (Philadelphia)

mad, glad

6) BE

iː > iːə / __ ɫ

feel [iː～iːəɫ], seal

② 単音化

BE の [eɪ oʊ aɪ aʊ ɔɪ] の第 2 要素が弱化、消失。そのため例えば sell : sail は対立しなくなる。

1) ʊə > ɔː

sure, poor

2) ʊə > uː / __r

とくに頻度の高い語で。

during, Jewry, jury, eureka, neurotic

   cf. gourd, Ruhr, bourse

2)′ ʊə > ɛː (East Anglian)

sure

3) ɔə > ɔː / __r, ɛə > ɛː / __r (限られた nonRP で)

pore, more, store, door, floor

fair, wear, tear, careful, bearing, care, where

4) { [aɪə] / [aʊə] } > [aə ɑə ɑːə] さらに [ɑː] へ。([ɑː] はとくに RP

で好まれる)

　　fire, desire, pirate, shire, admire

　　power, tower, our, flower, shower

5) eɪ, aɪ, ɔɪ はときに [eː aː ɔː]。とくに語末で。

　　player, try, joy, toy

5)′ eɪ > æː (East Anglia)

　　player

6) aɪ > ɪ

　　short-lived　元来 [aɪ] だが最近 [i] が使われる (BE, AE)。
　　long-lived
　　BE privacy [praɪ-]　12%
　　　　　　　　[prɪ-]　88%

7) əʊ > ɔ (EstE)

　　bolt, gold

(5) 中舌化

① oʊ > ʌʊ, əʊ

　　BE のほぼ完了した変化だが、若い人たちはさらに [ɛʊ] へ。
　　home, hope, stone, moment, over

② BE で無強勢音節の [ɪ ɒ ʌ e] > ə がみられる。[ɪ] は保守的とみられている。この傾向はとくに若い人たちの間で顕著である。ただし、完全母音を保つもの ((b)) もあるが、これらもいずれ中舌化へ向うかもしれない。

　　(a)　[ɪ]： system, blanket, captain, women, December, mistake, -ity (authority), -ace (surface), -ible (terrible), -ily (family), -ive (positive), be- (between), belong), enough, -ed (waited), -es (houses)

　　　　 [ɒ]： October, mosquito, boycott
　　　　 [ʌ]： sawdust

[e]： September

（b） possibly, private, -less (hopeless), engine, -ness (kindness), -ice (service), -age (message), -est (modest), de- (deserve), re- (remarkable)

(6) 脱落 (aphaeresis)
① 母音脱落
1) 語頭にある [ə], [ɪ] が無強勢音節で落ちる。これは口語体の特色。とくに V に先行されているとき (he 'scaped)、後ろに共鳴音 [＋sonorant C] を伴うとき好まれる。

[ə] 'bout, 'round, 'fraid, 'rrange, 'llow, 'pply, 'merican, 'head, 'shamed, 'nother, soon's ＜ soon as

[ɪ] 'nough, 'scape, 'leven

2) 語中

perhaps ＞ p'raps, H'lo, C'mon

② 音節脱落
1) VC

語頭にある無強勢音節 VC はあとに歯茎の歯擦音 ([s z]) がつづくとき脱落することがある。[s] の方が好まれる。あるいは I 'spect のように V、とくに 2 重母音が先行するときに起こる。削除されるコーダ (coda) はつづくオンセット (onset) と [ksp nst ksk] といった結合をつくる。

ɪg, ɪk： 'zactly, 'cept, 'spert

ɔːl： 'most

ɪn： 'stead, 'ept

ʌn： 'less

2) CV (C = 唇音まれに歯茎音、V = ə〜ɨ)

bɨ ： 'fore, 'cause (cause とつづる人もある), 'side

rɨ ： 'member, 'lief

tə	:	'mato
mə	:	'chine
sə	:	'ppose
hə	:	'Lo（＝hello）
də	:	dishevelled ＞ 'shevelled

15.4 綴字発音

20世紀に入ってからの大きな変化の要因の1つは綴字発音といってもよい。教育水準が上がり一般化されるにつれて綴字発音は重要な役を果すようになる。この現象はBEに多くAEに少ないのはすでにWebster以来発音と綴字を近づけようとする努力のゆえである。

① /C/

	BE	
often	t(27%)	φ(73%)（元来informalだったが最近formalな文脈でも。）
nephew	f(79%)	v(21%)
forehead	fɒrɪd〜fɔːhed(1920年代以降)	
waistcoat	weskɪt ＞ weɪstkəʊt	
Anthony	t〜θ	
Ipswich	dʒ ＞ tʃ(1930年代から tʃ)	
Horsham	s ＞ ʃ	
Greenwich	tʃ〜dʒ	
vehicle	víːɪk-〜víːh-	
toward	tɔːd ＞ təwɔːd	
Edward	édəd ＞ édwəd(19cから)	
quote	kəʊt ＞ kwəʊt(19cから)	
chivalry	tʃ ＞ ʃ	

calm, balm, palm (第2次大戦後 US, Canada で増えつつある。
　　　　　　　　ただし New England, Upstate NY などは
　　　　　　　　<l> を発音しない。)

② /V/

1) とくに目につくのは大陸式発音の採用で BE に顕著である。

　　eɪ > ɑː　　　gala, Copenhagen, armada, stratum,
　　　　　　　　apparatus, Alma Mater,
　　　　　　　　data [eɪ(92%), ɑː(6%), æ(2%)]
　　iː > eɪ　　　deity [eɪ(80%), iː(20%)], vehicle, homogeneity,
　　　　　　　　spontaneity
　　iː > e　　　ego
　　ʌ > ʊ　　　cum
　　aɪ > ɪ　　　alumni, dilemma (BE では [aɪ] がふつう)
　　ɔː > aʊ　　Faustus

2)
　　handkerchief　　　　ɪ > iː
　　comedy convent　　　ʌ > ɒ (8%-92%)
　　covert　　　　　　　ʌ > əʊ
　　lieutenant　　　　　1949年 lefte-(Army)～luːtê-(Navy); 1988
　　　　　　　　　　　　年 leften-
　　laundry　　　　　　 ɑː > ɔː
　　qualm　　　　　　　 ɔː > ɑː
　　patent　　　　　　　eɪ (一般的)～æ (とくに法律家)
　　-day　　　　　　　　eɪ (いい切りのとき)～i (あとに morning な
　　　　　　　　　　　　　　　　　　　　　どが起こるとき)
　　Mall　　　　　　　　1949年 æ～ɔː; 1988年 æ

3) BE speciality は AE specialty に影響をうけ3音節が聞かれる。

15.5 アクセント

単語のアクセントの揺れはいつの時代にも存在するが、どちらかというとAEよりもBEにおいて際立っている。

最近の傾向としては

- （ⅰ） 長い音節語は語頭よりも語末の方へ移す傾向がある。とくに語末から3音節目へ。
- （ⅱ） íncrease vs. incréase のようなアクセントによる品詞の区別は名詞型に統一しようとする努力が見られる。
- （ⅲ） アクセント推移は基体 (base) のアクセントをモデルとしていることがある。たとえば lámentabe でなく lamént の強勢を保持する laméntable を好む傾向に見られるように。
- （ⅳ） 複合語は AE ´ ` の影響で BE も ´ ` が増えてきているが、伝統的な ´ ` を守る。

    bédtime, Chrístmas card, móving van

15.5.1 揺れている項目

（1） ① 名詞関連の語

BE	AE
dischárge(N, V) > díscharge	díscharge
dispúte(62%), dís-(38%)	dispúte
reséarch(80%), résearch(20%) （増えつつある）	reséarch〜résearch
míscellany > miscéllany	míscellany
sùbmaríne(58%), súb-(42%)	sûbmarine〜sùbmaríne
addréss(N, V)	áddress(N), addréss(V)
garáge > gárage	garáge
adúlt > ádult〜adúlt	adúlt〜ádult

allóy > álloy   álloy～allóy
cigarét(85%), cígaret(15%)   cígaret～cigarét
magazíne   mágazine
áristocrat > arístocrat   arístocrat
conféssor   conféssor～cónfessor
allý(N)～álly   allý～álly
abdómen > ábdomen   ábdomen～abdómen
contróversy(56%), cóntroversy(44%)   cóntroversy
défect(86%), deféct(14%)   défect～deféct
fináncé   fínance～finánce
románce～rómance   románce～rómance
precédence > précedence   précedence～precédence
tránsference > transférence   transférence
láboratory > labóratory   láboratory
búreau～buréau   búreau
étiquette～etiquétte   étiquette
Ulýsses～Úlysses   Ulýsses～Úlysses
trajéctory～trájectory   trajéctory～trájectory
                                        (AE でも trajéctory がふつ
                                        うになりつつある)

kílometer(52%)   kiló-(48%)   kilómeter～kílometer
　(centimeter などへの類推で)

bállet   ballét～bállet
cáfe～café   café
clíche   cliché
fróntier～frontíer   frontíer
décade > decáde   décade～decáde
　② 形容詞、動詞関連の語

BE	AE
cómmunal(68%), commúnal(32%)	commúnal～cómmunal
décorous～decórous	décorous～decórous
sonórous ＞ sónorous	sonórous～sónorous
ímbecile～imbecíle	ímbecile
exquísite(69%), éxquisite(31%)	exquísite～éxquisite
hárass(68%), haráss(32%)	haráss～hárass

（後者は AE の影響で 1970 年代に使われるようになった）

BE	AE
cóntemplate～contémplate	cóntemplate
íllustrate～illústrate	íllustrate～illústrate
advertíse～ádvertise	ádvertise～advertíse
contríbute(73%), cóntribute(27%)	contríbute
dictáte(V)	díctate(V)～dictáte
vibráte	víbrate
rotáte	rótate

（2） 形容詞形成の接尾辞 -able, -ary, -ative を伴う形

BE	AE
applícable(77%), áppli-(23%)	ápplicable～applícable
formídable(54%), fórmidable(46%)	fórmidable～formídable
hospítable(81%), hósp-(19%)	hóspitable～hospítable
demónstrable(63%), démon-(37%)	demónstrable
dispútable～dísputable	dispútable～dísputable
frágmentary ＞ fragméntary	frágmentary
péjorative ＞ pejórative	pejórative～péjorative
éxplicable ＞ explícable	éxplicable～explícable
illústrative ＞ íllustrative	illústrative～íllustrative
préferable ＞ preférable	préferable～preférable
lámentable ＞ laméntable	laméntable～lámentable

(3) -ly 副詞

　　　　　　　　BE　　　　　　　　　　　　　　　AE

primárily(51%), prímar-(49%)　　　primárily〜prímarily

cónsequently　　　　　　　　　　　cónsequently〜consé-
　　　　　　　　　　　　　　　　　quently(FEN)

necessárily〜nécessarily　　　　　　necessárily〜nécessarily

(4) N vs. V のペア

　　最近の BE では V も ＿´＿ が増している。

　　　　　　　　BE　　　　　　　　　AE

annex　　N　＿´＿　　　　　　　　＿´＿
　　　　　V　＿＿´　　　　　　　　＿´＿ 〜 ＿＿´

contest　N　＿´＿　　　　　　　　＿´＿
　　　　　V　＿´＿ 〜 ＿＿´　　　＿´＿ 〜 ＿＿´

contrast　N　＿´＿　　　　　　　　＿´＿
　　　　　V　＿´＿ 〜 ＿＿´　　　＿´＿ 〜 ＿＿´

escort　　N　＿´＿　　　　　　　　＿´＿
　　　　　V　＿´＿ 〜 ＿＿´　　　＿´＿

export　　N　＿´＿　　　　　　　　＿´＿
　　　　　V　＿´＿ 〜 ＿＿´　　　＿´＿ 〜 ＿＿´

import　　N　＿´＿　　　　　　　　＿´＿
　　　　　V　＿＿´　　　　　　　　＿＿´

increase　N　＿´＿ 〜 ＿＿´　　　＿´＿ 〜 ＿＿´
　　　　　V　＿´＿ 〜 ＿＿´　　　＿´＿ 〜 ＿＿´
　　　　　(85%は V ＿＿´,
　　　　　N ＿´＿ の区別をする)

progress　N　＿´＿　　　　　　　　＿´＿
　　　　　V　＿´＿ 〜 ＿＿´　　　＿＿´

protest　　N　＿´＿　　　　　　　　＿´＿

15.5.2 リアルタイムの資料

(1) 20cに入って変化が終わったもの(BE)

Old	New
sonórous	sónorous
precédence	précedence
contémplate	cóntemplate
prematúre	prémature
artículatory	articulátory
éxplicable	explícable

(2) BE

1920	1949	1988	1990
adúlt			ádult ~adúlt
	artíficial ~ártificial	artíficial	
expért (A)			éxpert
	chúrchyárd	chúrchyard	
	cóld-blóoded	cold-blóoded	

súspect (A, N)　　　　　　　　　　　　　　　súspect
～suspéct

　　　　　　　gainsáy　　　　gàinsáy
　　　　　　　gállant　　　　 gállant
　　　　　　　 ～gallánt

(3)　AE
　　　　1930　　　　　　　1990
　　ádult　　　　　　adúlt～ádult
　　cóntroversy　　　cóntroversy
　　fórmidable　　　 fórmidable～formídable
　　lámentable　　　 laméntable～lámentable
　　reséarch (N)　　 reséarch～résearch

第 16 章　性差(sexism)

16.1　差別語

（1）　マイノリテイグループと女性の書きもの、ニューズ、公文書などの取り扱いの平等をめぐり、とくに 1964 年の公民権法(Civil Rights Act)施行によって、性差に基づく、好み、制約、差別を示すことばの使用を禁ずる動きが強まる。

イギリスでも最近、男女の差別語を使わなくなってきている。女性の同権闘争などの影響による。

① 人口調査局は 441 の労働カテゴリーを 52 に減らす(U. S. Department of Labor (1977) *Dictionary of Occupational Titles*)。

旧	新
airline stewardess	flight atttendant
fishermen	fishers
laundresses	launderers
firemen	firefighters
maid	house keeper
undertaker	grief counselor (Sanders *Trial* 3)

Connecticut 州では法律をつぎのように中性化する

　　　　wo/man　　s/he　　his/her

② これが出版界、ジャーナリズム、さらに一般に及ぶ。広告でも Help wanted―Male/Female となっていたものが Help wanted だけとなったりする。

英語では明らかに「女」を表すものが 220、「男」はわずか 22 しかない。

1) -ess

actress	actor
authoress	author
poetess	poet
waitress	(table)server, waitron, waitperson
hostess	host

2) -man / -master　　-woman / -mistress

salesman	salesperson
horseman	horsewoman
chairman	chairperson
schoolmaster	schoolmistress

3) lady/woman/girl

　　lady doctor
　　woman teacher
　　girl student

4)
housewife	housemaker, domestic partner(男・女)
mankind	humankind
women	womyn
history	herstory(女性史)
manpower	personpower(Sanders *Trial* 200)
	womanpower

5) Ms

　　AE では 70％が容認し、30％が認めていない (1975年)。タイトルで結婚の地位を示す習慣はずいぶん長い間の習慣で、早いころのアメリカでは未亡人は Widow Jones のようにいって自分の名はなかった。

　　Ms はこのような習慣への挑戦でもあって、とくに若い女性の間に急速に広まる。複数形は Mses。

　　Mrs/Misssh/Ms はいずれも Mistress の略で、17-18 c では Mrs が大人の女性の姓の前につけられていた (結婚、未婚をとわず)。Ms もまれながら同じように使われていた。Miss は female children に限られていた。18 c 末から Miss を既婚—未婚の区別に、19 c から Mrs を男のファーストネーム＋姓に「奥さん」であることを示す習慣が発達し始めた。

　　ただし、citizen, colleague, dealer, employee, expert, inhabitant, maker, operator, person, repairer, scientist, student, worker, writer などは性差がないのでそのまま使われるが、区別するときは woman/lady writer のようにいうことがある。

（2）差別語のいいかえはつぎのようなイディオム、格言にも及ぶ (cf. Maggio 1991)。

act like a man ＞ meet danger, take heart, stand tall, etc.
All work and no play makes *Jack* a dull boy ／ before you can say *Jack Robinson* ／ *Boys* will be *boys* ／ The child is father of *the man*
　　cf. the kids were being kids　　　　　(Grisham *Client* 91)
しかし Can we have a *man*-to-*man* talk ? (子供が母親へ) のようなイディオムや *man*hole などでは単なるいいかえで定着するかどうかは不明である。また、a *sister* city ／ a *mother* country ／ a *mother* tongue ／ *mother*fucker ／ *Mother* Goose なども同様である。

(コーパスによる調査)

	-woman	-man
spokes-	少し	圧倒的に多い
chair-	ほとんど	圧倒的に多い
business-	少し	多い

これは男性がまだ権力・権威の座にずっと多くいることを示す。

(3) 代名詞の問題

① everyone / -body / a person / nobody / no one / someone などを he / she で受ける問題。

1) they / their / them を用いることによって避ける。

2) 不格好だが he or she, his or her, s/he, he/she, his/her を用いる。

3) 新しい代名詞：E/hesh を用いる。

男性語で女性も含む表現を男性中心語(androcentric)―例えば he―という。

② つぎの名詞は代名詞で受けるとき直感的に he / she いずれかで受けることが多い。

policeman, doctor, president, sailor, professor は *he* で、nurse, elementary school teacher, secretary, baby-sitter, house-keeper は *she* で受けることが多い。子供の読物では he が she の3倍も使われている。動物を受けるときも he がふつうである。

③ 語順の問題(受け入れられていないが順序を入れ替えよと主張する人がいる)

boys and girls (半分 girls and boys とすべきとする人あり)

Mr & Mrs / husband and wife / male and female / man and wife / ladies and gentlemen

 cf. mother and father〜father and mother / Romeo and Juliet / Anthony and Cleopatra / Jack and Jill / 太郎と花子

16.2 男・女性語と意味

（1） lady—gentleman　woman—man　girl—boy

① 今日ではこの対立は残して、lady はしばしば man の対語となる。相手を man といっても失礼とならないが woman というとそうなるので lady は woman の婉曲(euphemism)となり、adult female を表す無標(UM)な語となる。

　また、しばしば低い職業やつまらない行為について用いられさえする。
sales ladies ／ ladies' wear, men's wear ／ cleanly lady ／ act like a lady(子供へのこごと) ／ here's a lady at the door
lady は sexuality を含意せず purity, elegance を含意するのに対して woman は sexual maturity を含意する。

　なお、woman は Victoria 朝では 'paramour' の意味だったので female がとって代わり、さらに lady へとって代わった。

　一方、man は UM な語で gentleman はその特定タイプを指す。

② girl ／ gal も大人について使われ(two men and two girls)、しばしば offensive の意味を含むので、ここでも lady が使われることがある。また、middle or late teen の少女をさすとき maturity が欠けている意味にも使われる。

③ 年令のイメージ調査(数字は%)

　lady：　　　　adult(18%), 大卒(44%), mature woman(36%)
　gentleman：　 young adult(31%), middle adult(55%), older man (12%)
　woman：　　　adult(65%), mature female(30%)
　man：　　　　teen(11%), adult(51%), mature male(38%)
　girl：　　　　mid-adolescent(20%), older adolescent(31%), young adult(35%), young mature(14%)

boy: older child(28%), young adolescent(39%), mid-adolescent(33%)

（2）男性語に比べて女性語は時間の経過とともに悪化し、しばしば「ばとう語」として用いられる。

① prostitute を表す語は 500 に上るが、whore monger は 65 のみ。

pro(M): 'competent' player ／ pro(F): 'prostitute'

tramp(M): 'drifter' ／ tamp(F): 'prostitute'

buddy(愛情を込めた意で「親友」) ＜ brother ／ sissy(軽蔑的な意で) ＜ sis(ter)＋y

call boy[＝page] ／ call girl(1900 年から)

baggage(だらしない売春婦) ／ doxy ／ pavement princess ／ trollope, etc.

② queen ／ madam ／ mistress(EModE) ／ spinster ／ niece(私生児) ／ aunt(年取った売春婦) ／ crone(しわくちゃばばあ) ／ bag(みにくい女) ／ wench

cf. prince ／ king ／ lord ／ father ／ bachelor ／ uncle ／ brother ／ nephew

（3）動物・鳥・食物

① 動物

M: ape(粗野な男), buck[＝youth], bull(大男；ポリ)

F: bat[＝prostitute], beast[＝prostitute], bird(あま), cat(意地悪女), dog(つまらん女；prostitute), pig(だらしない女；ポリ), pussy(女), vixen(がみがみ女), cow(だらしない女), trot(売春婦), heifer(めす), sow(めす), shrew(ねずみ ＞ がみがみ女)

M, F: lamb(ポリ), fox(魅力的な女(若者)), ox(鈍重な人)

② 食物名

M: beefcake, cookie, pudding(太っちょ)

F: cheesecake, peach, sweet(いとしい人；恋人), pie(女), tomato

(少女；prostitute)
M, F： fruit(ホモの男；女の子), fruit cake(ホモの男), honey(妻・夫・子供へ), sugar(妻・夫へ)

16.3 職業と男女差(アメリカ)

1989、1990年の統計(Time)では女性の56％、59％、男性の49％、65％はアメリカ社会は男社会だとする。

① teacher
preschool(保育園)、kindergartenの先生の98％
elementary schoolの先生の85％が女性で、一方、
public school 管理職の96％、
public school 校長の76％(白人 90％)、
college / university の教師の62％は男性である。

② policemanの13％が女性である。

③ armed forces
200万のうち11％が女性である。
top officer(上級将校)は2％以下、
brigadier general(准将―大佐と少将の間)およびそれ以上は1％以下が女性である。

④ 1990年のアメリカ統計によると1000の大会社のexecutives(役職者)中manager(管理者)の5％以下が女性、またはminoritiesである。1989年の女性の月給取りは130万人、男性は1460万人である。

16.4 男・女ことばのちがい

(1) conversational style
① ぼかし表現(hedge)

I think / I'm sure / you know / sort of / kind of / I guess：
女性の方が使うことが多い。とくに不安というよりも confidence, certainty を表すときに多い。

また、今しゃべっている人を支持するために短い反応(minimal responses)を適切にはさむ。

② verbosity

女性は男性よりもしゃべる時間が短くおしゃべりではない。

③ topic shift

男性が OK、Oh well といった間投詞(interjection)を topic shift にするのに対し、女性は接続詞(conjunction)を使うことが多い。

④ silence

女性間では分布は5分5分であるのに対し、
男女間では大部分は女性である。

⑤ compliments

女性の方が与えることが多く、またそれを受けることが多い。

⑥ 丁重さ(politeness)

女性が多い。Would you please / I'd really appreciate it if〜

⑦ 数字

女性は男性よりも数字を使わない。使うときも about / around / or などをつける。

⑧ 誓い(swearing) / タブー(taboo)

男性の方が多用する。例えば、漫画でも male characters はしばしば swear する。ただ男性も女性といっしょだと頻度が落ちる。

taboo は最近女性もかなり幅広く使う傾向にある(damn)。

(2) 手紙のあいさつに現れる男・女差
① 未知の人へは性にかまわずに Dear Sir / Gentleman を用いる。
② しかし、両性を含む Dear friends / folk / people とすべきだという意見もあって最近増えている。Dear Manager/Publisher/Reader/

Editor/Friend(s) of the Library のように男女を含むいい方を用いる。

また、business letter など人によっては salutation を省き本文を始めるものもみられる。そして、帰結部もやめてしまうこともある。

(3) 台風名

1970年代は Hurricane Eloise のように女性名をつけたがそれ以降は男女交替で用いられる。

(4) 男・女の子のことばの習得

一般に少女の方が男の子よりも習得が早く優れている。これは 10〜11才ぐらいでもことばの理解、語彙の多さ、助動詞のような複雑な表現の扱いでもすぐれている。これは少女が母親と積極的に接触するためであろう。

発音も小さいうちから性によるちがいが存在する。New England の村の子の場合 <ing> ［iŋ］(少女) vs.［in］(少年)の傾向がみられる。

Scotland の少女は［ɹ］を好み r-なしをさけるが、男の子は［ɾ］、r-なしを使う。少女は年をとるにつれて非標準形をさけ、標準形へ向うが、男の子は非標準形を positive value ありと考えそれを強化する。

第 17 章　婉曲 (euphemism)

　多くの民族において、タブー視される(社会的に受け入れられない)出来事、事物、性格などはしばしば他のやわらかないいかえによって表される。しかしそれもすぐに婉曲性を失って別の語にとって代わられていく。
　最近の傾向はかなり直截的、blunt にいう傾向が強い。一般に男性のほうがそうである。150 年ぐらい前では英米とも leg, breast は foot, bosom といって避けられていた。roast chicken, Thanksgiving turkey も今日でも残るように white meat, dark meat といった。

① 死、病気などのことばの上のタブー
　(ⅰ) pass away / leave the world / go west / join the great majority
　(ⅱ) pregnant : expecting

② 社会的モラル上のタブー (obscenities ; profanity (神の冒瀆))
　(ⅰ) sex :
　　　元来 sexual intercourse は婉曲的ないい方だったが、bed with / sleep with / go to bed with / make love to / have sex with さらに、have an affair / go out with / I was out with Tony
　　　俗語 : shag, bonk (英)
　　　4文字語 : cock / fuck / cunt / pussy / screw / tits / balls

I don't allow the F word　　　　　　　　　(Archer)

fuck は最初 1936 年英語辞典に収録されたが学校、図書館などで嵐のような非難を招く。1959 年 D. H. Lawrence : *Lady Chatterley's Lover* がアメリカで出版されるとさらに大きな反響をまきおこし、発禁となる。英米とも裁判に入るが、イギリスで 1960 年無罪判決が出たことで文学作品などでは許容されるに至る。しかし 4 文字語としていまでも強い反対がある。

（ⅱ）toilet、排泄：

WC / loo / toilet / wash one's hands / powder room / ladies' (gentlemen's) room / go to the john

文脈によっては Will you excuse me？

a rest room / a comfort station / use the little girl's room

urine / shit / piss

③ 知能などの遅れ、身体上の欠陥などを直截的にからかって別語でいうこと、たとえば fool を goose / cuckoo / donkey / goof / pigeon という例や、弱者へのおもいやり―政治的公正 (political correctness (PC))―は、とくにアメリカでは盛んである。イギリスでも、教養のある人たちは racist, sexist, ageist 的なことをのべることは受け入れないが、方言発音についての失礼な態度は PC に反すると考えられていない。

　　cf.　PC 1975 invented by Karen deCrow (National Organization for Women の会長)。Henry Beard & C. Cerf (1993) : *The Official Politically Correct Dictionary and Handbook*。

old　　　　　chronologically gifted

poor　　　　economically marginalized (poor ＞ needy ＞ deprived ＞ underprivileged ＞ disadvantaged のように bad condition になると変わっていく)

fat　　　　　horizontally challenged

第 17 章　婉曲 (euphemism)　165

　　　short　　　　　　vertically challenged
　　　disabled　　　　 physically challenged
　　　dead　　　　　　terminally inconvenienced
　　　deaf　　　　　　 hearing-impaired
　　　foolish　　　　　intellectually handicapped / ungifted / weak-headed / mentally deficient / backward educated / deficient / defective
　　cf.　日本語　つんぼ/めくら/ばか(知的障害名)

④　人種名

（ⅰ）人種起源を示す名前は、皮膚の色、居住地域、職業、宗教など社会的区別の要因となる。とくにアメリカではそうで、例えば、Irish potato 飢饉のときはアイルランド人に対し、McKinley 大統領がポーランド人に殺されたときはポーランド人に、2つの大戦では German-American, Japanese-American に、さらに、NYにおける Mafia のゆえに Italian が、また、東部の Puerto Rican, Cuban, Southwest の Mexican-American、黒人、東洋人、ユダヤ人などが対象となる。

　　Indian > Native American
　　Black > Colored > Negroes > Black > Afro-American > African American

（ⅱ）また個人名が生国名では英語の音声型にあらわれないという理由で変えられたり、誤った発音が定着したりする。これも1種の差別。

　　スペイン人名　　　Santos > sǽntəs
　　ポーランド人名　　Kwiatkowçki > kəwátski:
　　　　　　　　　　　Italian > tye-talian
　　　　　　　　　　　Arab > éiræb

⑤　宗教的タブー (profanities) 憎悪、敬意、おちこみ、驚きを表す。

(ⅰ) God　goy(1350) / 'sblown(1598) / zounds ［＝ god's wounds］(1600) / gad(1611) / golly(1743) / gracious(1760) / by George(1842) / Drat(1844) / by gad / by golly / oh my

　　　Jesus　Gee(1925)

　　　Lord　Lud(1725) / Lor(1835)

(ⅱ) 1989年の判決以降特定宗教、例えば、キリスト教のおしつけは差別になるということで、公的な場でも宗教的表示等はさけられ、Christmas も Holiday に置換しつつある。それはキリスト教だけでなくヒンズー教、ユダヤ教、イスラム教、仏教などが存在するため。

　　　Christmas tree ＞ Holiday tree

　　　Christmas gift ＞ Holiday gift

第 18 章　誓い（swearing）・罵倒

元来は神への祈りによって厳粛な「誓い」をいった（take an oath）。のち、「絶対に、本当に」といった強調、のろい（expletive）の表現を発達、神への冒瀆、きたないことばとなる。日本語、アメリカインディアンなどは誓いをしない。

（1）誓い

「神」にかけて誓うのがふつう。ただ God や神のいる天にかけてはならないとする聖書に反するので、God をいろいろいいかえて使う。なお、古代 Ionia では「キャベツにかけて」（二日酔いのさまし薬としてのキャベツ）、ソクラテスは「犬にかけて」、ピタゴラスは「4 にかけて」といった。

My God / gosh / golly

My Lord / land / law

Jesus / gee (Gee this) / jees

Christ / crickey

I swear *on my mother's life* I didn't do it.

　　cf. 日本語「後生だから」、「首にかけて、首をやる」

（2）のろい、強調

性、排泄などタブー視されている語句を用いる。なお、AE ののろい

のことばは 17 c の BE から入っていったものが多い。

① 性、排泄

fuck（起源不明。16 c 初めに。のろいには 20 c 初めから。）
eff (1952)　fucker (男・女)　prick (男)　cunt (女)
tit (女)　shit (1934)　sherbet (1934)　ass　arse　asshole (男・女)
bitch (女)

What the fuck...?　　Fuck me !　　Fuck it !
Kick off your buttocks.

② hell / damn

 (ⅰ) hell

とくに AE で 1930 年以降盛んになった。

1) 否定の副詞として、あるいはその強意語 (intensifier) として：Like *hell* I will〔= I will *never* do〕

2) 強意の副詞として：...hate like *hell*

3) 疑問詞の強意語として：What the *hell* ?

4) 断言の強意語：*Hell,* yes !

5) hell of a + N で「すごい、とんでもない」

You're doing a great job.　You're one *hell* of a secretary !

(Sheldon *Morning* 126)

hell のやわらかい形として heck が用いられる。

 (ⅱ) damn / damned

今日では hell よりも盛んである。良い意味にも用いる。damn の代わりに drat, blast (とくに BE), darn ともいう。damned の代わりに blamed, blowed ともいう。damn に対して d＿＿＿, damned に対して d＿＿d も使われる。

Damn (it) !　　God damn (it) !

I'm the best *damned* player in the world.

damn のやわらかい形として dash (d＿ と書くことから来ている)

が用いられる。

（iii）その他

1) pig（男）　cow（女）　doggone
2) son of (a) bitch（男）

   sonofabitch ともつづられる。son of a gun ともいう。

   bitch は元来男・女だったがのち女に。harlot も同じ。sow（女）bastard（男・女）。
3) rotten, rubbish
4) bloody

   最初 18 c 後半に Samuel Foote の作品の中で she's a *bloody* fine girl とした bloody がはやり、その後 bl- 語としてきらわれ、obscene ないしは profane な語として Victoria 朝には禁句であったが（代わりに blasted / blinking / blooming などが使われた）1913 年 Bernard Shaw の作品 *Pygmalion* で Eliza に使わせたときはすごい反響をまき起こした。

   the *bloody* marvelous singer

   It's *bloody* raining

（iv）まんがの swearing の例（1935 年～）

   読者を傷つけないようにやわらかないい方：

   hot dog / good gosh / My gosh / Oh gee / Heavens! / Good heaven / Heavenly Day

   強い profanity の代用：

   Lawzy [= lousy] / Golley (< God) / Drat (< Go*d r*ot) / Darn (< damn)

   俗語的用法：Phonie!

第19章　丁重さ(politeness)

（１）丁重さのメカニズム
① 丁重さには(ⅰ)顔(face)、(ⅱ)力(power)が関係する。
respect face は他人の feelings へ同情を示すことで
　　（ａ）　強制されない顔(negative face)と
　　（ｂ）　好かれたり、賛美されたりする必要のある顔(positive face)が
　　　　　ある。
power　不均衡な相対的な力関係
　　　　　一般に話手は相手よりも多少 powerful になる。
相手の positive face の要求に対して、あいさつしたり、ほめたり(You look nice)して満足させる。
　一方 negative face の要求に対しては、協力しなくてもよく、いいわけをもって断ることがある(I'm awfully sorry but I can't help you)。
② 女性は自分のしゃべっていることが相手の顔をおびやかすかもしれないと他人の顔の要求に敏感に気づいていて、いろいろなことばを使う。そこで積極的な丁重さとして、I {sincerely / really} {assert / request / promise} といった強い particle を用いる。消極的な丁重さとして、I {tentatively / maybe} {assert / request} といった表

現を用いて丁重さを示す。

　　一方、男性はずっと matter-of-fact 調を用いることが多い。

　　ただし、I respectfully decline は丁重さはなく、抗議、拒否を表すことが多い。

(2) いろいろな丁重さのストラッタジー

① 一般に語数が多いほど丁重さは増す。

please を用いる (please explain it)

② 助動詞の過去形

Could you explain it?

Would you mind...?

I couldn't agree with you more [=I perfectly agree with you]

③ 疑問文/否定文

I wonder if〜 / Could you explain it?

否定文：いいわけや賛意を示すとき

I wouldn't be surprised if〜

BE では kindly, be so good as to を用いても命令形では丁寧さはない。

Be so good as to do it for me.

④ その他

(ⅰ) yes ＞ yeah をきらって definitely (若い層), precisely, quite (高年齢層) が用いられる。no の代わりに not really がよく使われる (BE)。

(ⅱ) お礼のいい方

thank you ＞ thank you {very much / a lot} ＞ thank you very much indeed...

最近 AE で thank you much が聞かれる。

(3) 2人称単数・複数代名詞による丁重さ

標準英語では 18c にこの区別が消えたがいまでもなお England 北部

の1部で保持され、ここでは上位、年上には you で、少年や年下のものの男同士では thou が使われる。

ME, EModE	thou	ye, you
フランス語	tu	vous
ドイツ語	du	Sie
ラテン語	tu	vos
ロシア語	ty	vy
イタリア語	tu	Lei
スウェーデン語	du	ni
ギリシャ語	esi	esis

第20章　呼び掛け・名前

　呼び掛けの称号(title)、名前(姓(Last Name；以下LN)・名(First Name；以下FN)の使用、あいさつなどは話手と聞手の関係により決まる：(i)地位、(ii)親密さの度合い。
- ① 英語では称号＋LN あるいは FN を互いに使い合わないのは力の不均衡を示す。
- ② 互いに称号＋LN を使うのは不平等、不慣れを示す。
- ③ 互いに FN を使うのは対等、親しさを示す。
- ④ 称号だけで呼び掛けるのはもっとも親しさに欠けるとき(Doctor / Colonel)。
- ⑤ FN で呼び掛けるのは相手に親しさを表すか、力を assert するかである。
- ⑥ 医者は初診でも女性には FN を、男性には称号＋LN を用いる。

（1）親—子
　　　father-in-law(mother-in-law)への呼び掛けはむずかしく
　　　Mr Smith では too formal, Bill では too familiar, Dad では unnatural である。
　　　しかし孫が生まれると Grandad が用いられる。
　　　Since I'm going to be your father-in-law let's get off this 'sir'

business. Call me Alex.—Right, Alex.　　(Sheldon *Nothing* 309)
　　　cf. 日本やヌエル(Nuer)族(アフリカの種族)では kinship term (father / uncle / older sister など)をそのまま呼び掛けに用いる。
(2) 結婚と称号
　① 英語圏では女性は結婚すると自分の名を先に、男の名を LN とする。ただしスコットランドでは公文書にはもとの LN と新しい LN を記録する。しかし、今日のように長寿でかつ何回も結婚する時代、あるいは nonsexism がさけばれる時代では名前の扱いや称号が問題となる(⇒ 16 章性差)。
　② 夫婦別姓
　　　元来日本は別姓だったが戦国武士が現れ、下克上の時代になると姓を自分でつけた。また、姓のない妻女も夫の名をつけるようになる。そして夫婦同姓が一般化していく。
　　　とくに中国では昔から今日にいたるまで別姓とする。
　③ スペイン語圏では女性は自分の名のあとに夫の名をつける(Julia Martinez > Julia Martinez de Gomez)。
(3) 学界/学術論文と称号
　　　nickname をさけ、Mr よりも Dr のような大げさな title を好む機関もあれば、Mr Mrs Miss を好む機関もある。
　　　学術論文では男に refer するときは LN、女性に refer するときは Jane Dove といったり、Miss Dove といったりする。最近は性の区別なく LN のみを用いる傾向が強い。
(4) 称号の使用と地域性
　　　ヨーロッパ、メキシコ、ラテンアメリカなどではこみ入った称号使用がみられる。例えば、ドイツでは Herr Professor Doktor, Frau Professor Doktor のように3つのタイトルを用いる。ドイツ、フランスでも Herr Professor Potter / Mousieur le Professor Potter と

2つ用いる。

　英国の Victoria 朝では妻が夫を Mr Smith / Dr Smith と呼ぶことがあったが今は FN あるいは愛称(honey)を用いる。

1970年代の BE の呼び掛け

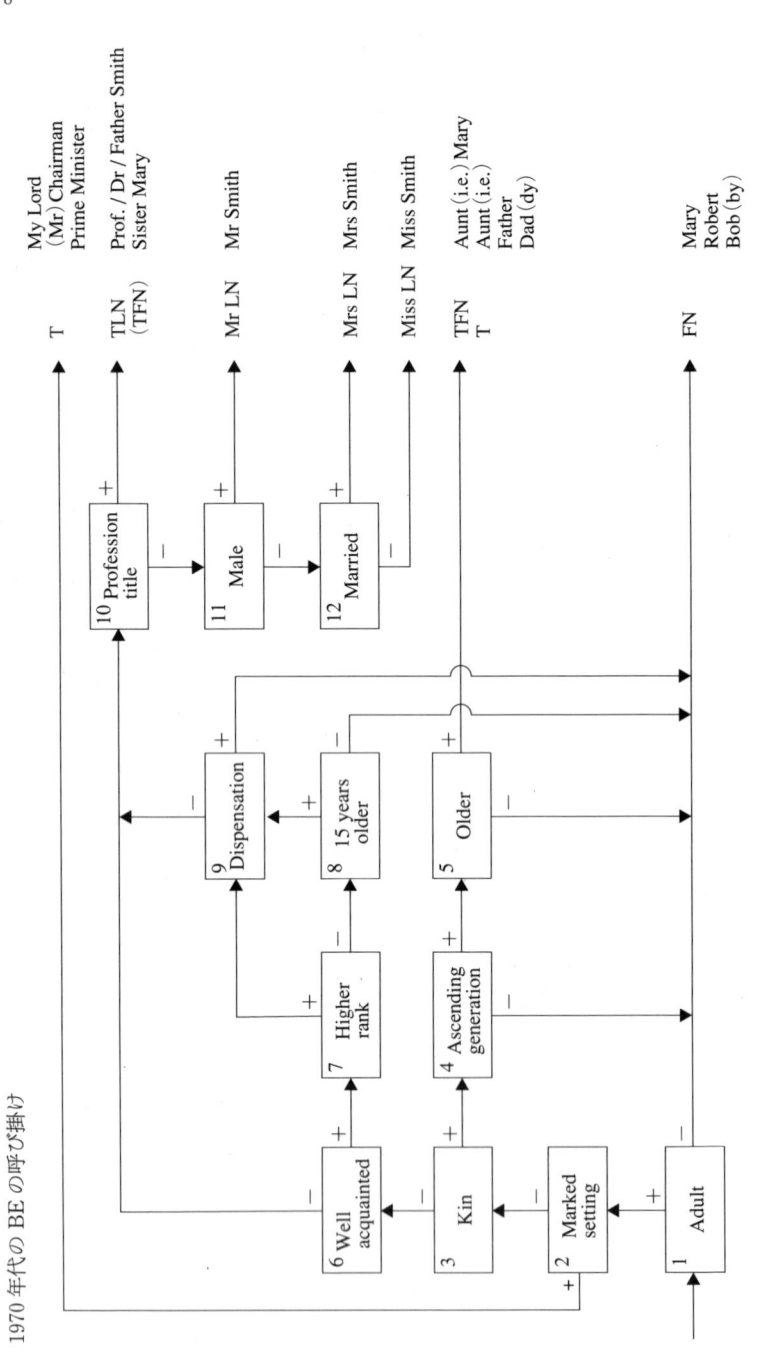

Factors constraining the polite choice of address terms in British English. (Reproduced from Laver 1981 : 297)

第 21 章　結論

過去数世紀にまたがって起ってきたことばの変化は 20 世紀に入って slow down したようにみえる。21 世紀の英語は、今世紀の変化を引き継ぎ、一定の方向、一定の幅、一定の channel 内を進むことになろう。

その変化は一言でいえば、制約、不規則性を最小化、すなわち、規則性を最大化し、深いレベルで幼児のことばの習得を容易にする簡単な文法をもつことばへ進む。

以下 21 世紀の英語の進む方向、姿を求めて述べてみる。

（１）　英語の拡大

①　　英語は 18-19 世紀までそれほど広く使われていなかった。最初 England、東南部スコットランド、中世に入って他のスコットランドの部分へ、16 c 以降 Wales、Ireland、18 c 以降北部 Ireland、北米へ拡がった。北米ではスペイン、オランダ、スウェーデンから領土を手中にし、英語の拡大に一役買った。

　　　18-19 c に入ると South Africa, Australia, New Zealand、さらに India、18 c に France が入り込んでいた Canada へ拡がっていった。

②　　一方、植民地化に伴い英語を基礎としたピジン、クリオールが、Atlantic pidgins, Caribbean Creoles, St Helena, West Africa, Papua New Guinea, Solomons Island, New Hebrides などで発達した。

The Spread of English

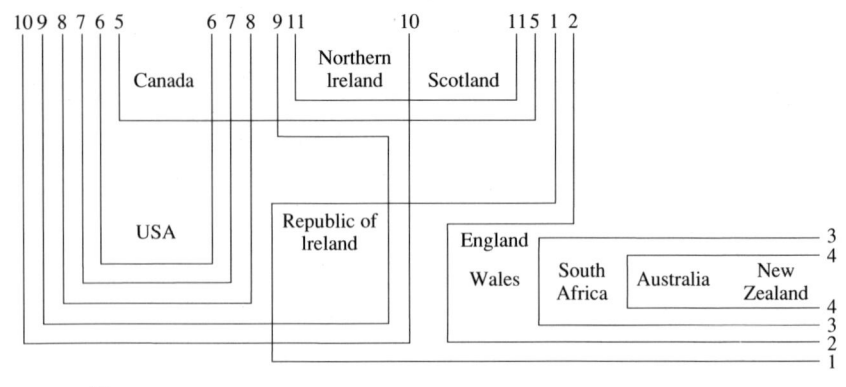

```
10 9 8 7 6 5      6 7 8  9 11      10        11 5 1 2
                         Northern
            Canada       Ireland   Scotland

                  Republic of                                           3
            USA   Ireland         England                               4
                                  Wales   South   Australia   New
                                          Africa              Zealand
                                                                        4
                                                                        3
                                                                        2
                                                                        1
```

Key
1. /ɑː/rather than /æ/in *path etc.*
2. absence of non-prevocalic /r/
3. close vowels for /æ/and/ɛ/, monophthongization of /ai/and/au/
4. front [aː] for /ɑ:/in *part etc.*
5. absence of contrast of /ɒ/ and/ɔː/as in *cot* and *caught*
6. /æ/rather than /ɑː/ in *can't* etc.
7. absence of contrast of /ɒ/ and /ɑː/ as in *bother* and *father*
8. consistent voicing of intervocalic /t/
9. unrounded [ɑ] in *pot*
10. syllabic /r/ in *bird*
11. absence of contrast of /ʊ/ and /uː/ as in *pull* and *pool*

(Trudgill & Hannah 1994:6)

（2） 今日の英語とこれからの英語
　① 今日の英語
　　（ⅰ） 第1言語として約3億人(cf. スペイン語　2億1千万、フランス語　1億9千万、アラビア語　1億8千万)、公用とする国で2億5千万人。
　　　　アメリカ、イギリス、オーストラリア、カナダ、ニュージーランドなどの国ぐにで。
　　　　第2言語として約3億人(フィリピン)

　　　　　外国語として学ぶ人約1億人(日本)
（ⅱ）　交易語として第1位
（ⅲ）　学術出版物　医学関係の7割
　　　　　　　　　　物理学の9割
（ⅳ）　出版本　世界の5分の1
（ⅴ）　高等教育、国際貿易、銀行業務、国際関係、会議、旅行、大衆文化、音楽、映画など
（ⅵ）　外交、航空、放送

　このように英語は商業、産業、科学、技術、政治、電子メディア(例えばinternet)を含むマスメディアなどで、民族から独立して(どういう形の社会的規制からも自由な)国際補助言語として重要な地位を占めつづけるであろう。

　国際的な情況の要求を満たす新しい型の英語、World Standard Spoken English(Crystal 1997:137)、これに影響を与えるのはAEであろう。

② これからの英語

　かってH. Sweetが1877年から1世紀後にはBE, AE, AustEはそれぞれ独立の発音変化のために互いに理解できないことばをしゃべっていることになろうと予言した。しかし、国際的TV番組や新聞、テキスト、他の印刷物などにおける標準英語のためにちがいを小さくした。

　21世紀には、現在存在する2つの大きな自律的versionの一方である北米英語(AE, CanadianE)へ、もう一方のversionであるイギリス英語(BE, AustE, New ZealandE, South AfricanE)が、同一出版物の両versionでの出版、旅行、映画、電話等によって、両者間にみられるとくに発音と語彙のギャップを埋めながら接近する(想像以上にAEによるBEへの影響、接近がみられる)。

　この「新英語」は、アメリカの経済力、政治力、技術力、先端科学

などを背景にして、国際的なコミュニケーション語としてますます重要性を増していく。

標準英語と他の変種との差の大きいイギリス英語でも、地理的、階級的な変異を標準英語がますます取り入れ、口語的(informal)な性格を強めていく。そしていっそうアメリカ英語の取り入れへの抵抗を弱めていく。

（3） 英語の将来と AE（Crystal 1997:117 ff）

英語の未来は US の未来とかなり関係する。事実 20 c の間の英語の成長を促進した力の多くは US に由来する。(ⅰ)英語の話手は他の国の 4 倍もの母語話者をもつ。(ⅱ)20c の technology の国際的発達に大きく係わってきた。とくに electronic revolution の支配。

ことばと力―軍事、経済―は密接な関係があるから、21c でも US の力による英語の拡大が見込まれよう―US 内で互いの intelligibility と元来の母国の identity のかっとうは続くにせよ、英語は social adhesive つまり政治的統一を保証することばの「接着剤(glue)」となろう。

（4） これからの英語の特徴
  ① 発音
  発音変異をなるべく余剰的にして統一していこうという傾向がみられる。これは交通、電話、映画、舞台、TV、ラジオ放送、教育の一般化、さらに辞書を含む出版等の影響を受ける。
  （ⅰ） i, u の 2 重母音化
  ② 文法
  （ⅰ） 動詞・副詞結合(give out, give in, get up)の発達
  （ⅱ） VT ↔ VI の交替。とくに他動詞化の傾向一層強まる。
  （ⅲ） 進行形、受身の制約がますます弱まる。文語では受身が好まれる。
  （ⅳ） He's better than *me* / It's *me*

- （ⅴ）懸垂分詞（dangling participle）の許容
- （ⅵ）省略（主語、動詞、冠詞、前置詞、接続詞）
  That one over there?
- （ⅶ）平叙文が増し、命令文や感嘆文は少なくなっていく（文語）
- （ⅷ）動名詞、不定詞、分詞構文が好まれる（文語）
- （ⅸ）補文（complement clause）が多い（文語）
- （ⅹ）口語では過去形が、文語では現在完了が好まれる

③ 語形
- （ⅰ）不規則動詞の規則動詞化
- （ⅱ）所有格、複数、代名詞の格、時制、比較の接辞などユニークなものは残るが、可能なものは規則化される方向へ。その代わりに統語関係につよく依存する。

④ 語形成
- （ⅰ）ゼロ派生が盛んとなる。

⑤ 意味
- （ⅰ）ふつうの語の多重化
  rough には45ほどの意味がある［＝uneven, rugged, rude, etc.］。
  make up には14ほどの意味がある［＝constitute, invent, dress, decide, etc.］。
- （ⅱ）古い語（句）に新しい俗語的意味が付与されたり、廃語が復活したりする。専門語が一般化され、古語（例えば amplex）が新しい専門の意味をもったりする。

⑥ 語彙
- （ⅰ）OEは約35,000といわれているので、PEで約14倍の50万にふくれ上がっている。
  科学、マスメディアで語彙は急増しつづける。
  よく使われる語：infrastructure / ecosystem / senior citizen / bottom line / couch potato / in the

framework of / interface / lifestyle / parameter / scenario / syndrome / visibility / window of opportunity

(ⅱ) 口語的(informal)、俗語的(slang)、あるいはタブーとされた表現が使われていく。

horribly / absolutely / brilliant / great / super

(ⅲ) 口語では単音節語が好まれる。文語では多音節語が好まれる。

(ⅳ) 古語の revival

toll / rue the day / albeit / uncouth / thrice
would as soon forget　　　　　　　　(Hailey *Airport* 149)

出典一覧

Archer, Jeffrey
    Accidents : A Chapter of Accidents
    Christina : Christina Rosenthal
    First : First among Equals
    4th : The Fourth Estate
    Hiccup : Henny's Hiccup
    K&A : Kane and Abel
    Matter : A Matter of Honor
    Principle : A Matter of Principle
    Prod : The Prodigal Daughter
    Steal : The Steal
    Thieves : Honor among Thieves

Block, Laurence
    Closet : The Burglar in the Closet
    Hit : Hit Man
    Kipling : The Burglar who Liked to Quote Kipling
    Topless : The Topless Tulip Caper
    Williams : The Burglar who Traded Ted Williams

Cornwell, Patricia
    All : All that Remains
    Body : The Body Farm
    Potter's : From Potter's Field

Unnatural : Unnatural Exposure
Unusual : Cruel and Unusual

Crichton, Michael
 Disclosure : Disclosure
 Rising : Rising Sun

Dickey, Eric J.
 Friends : Friends and Lovers
 Sister : Sister Sister

Drabble, Margaret
 Curtain : Curtain
 Waterfall : Waterfall
 Year : Garrik Year

Dunning, John
 Booked : Booked to Die

Forsyth, Frederick
 Jackal : The Day of the Jackal

Grisham, John
 Chamber : The Chamber
 Client : The Client
 Rainmaker : The Rainmaker
 Runaway : The Runaway Jury
 Time : A Time to Kill

Hailey, Arthur
    Airport : Airport
    Detective : Detective
    Hotel : Hotel
    Wheels : Wheels

Klavan, Andrew
    Crime : True Crime

Koontz, Dean
    Face : The Face of Fear
    Fear : Fear Nothing
    Intensity : Intensity
    Moon : Winter Moon
    Murder : Mr. Murder
    Strangers : Strangers
    Survivor : Sole Survivor
    Watchers : Watchers

Parker, Robert B.
    Vices : Small Vices

Rice, Anne
    Vampire : The Vampire Lestat

Robbins, Harold
    Betsy : The Betsy
    Goodbye : Goodbye, Janette
    Lady : The Lovely Lady
    Love : Where Love Has Gone

Memories : Memories of Another Day
Merchants : The Dream Merchants
Pred : The Predators
Spellbinder : Spellbinder
Stallion : Stallion
Stiletto : Stiletto
Storyteller : The Storyteller
Stranger : Never Love a Stranger
Xanadu : Descent from Xanadu

Sanders, Laurence
   Luck : McNally's Luck
   Pleasures : Guilty Pleasures
   Puzzle : McNally's Puzzle
   Risk : McNally's Risk
   Secret : McNally's Secret
   Trial : McNally's Trial

Sheldon, Sidney
   Bloodline : Bloodline
   Doomsday : The Doomsday Conspiracy
   Dreams : Tell me your Dreams
   Game : Master of the Game
   Memories : Memories of Midnight
   Morning : Morning, Noon and Night
   Naked : The Naked Face
   Nothing : Nothing Lasts Forever
   Other : The Other Side of Midnight
   Rage : Rage of Angels
   Sands : The Sands of Time

Stars : The Stars Shine Down
Stranger : A Stranger in the Mirror
Windmills : Windmills of the Gods

Simon, Neil
 Little : Little me
 Red : Last of the Red Hit Lovers
 Windmills : Windmills

Steel, Danielle
 Ghost : The Ghost
 Gift : The Gift
 Love : To Love Again
 Paris : Five Days in Paris
 Passion : Season of Passion

Winchester, Simon
 Prof : The Professor and Madman

参考文献(*は辞書類)

Aarts, B. and C. F. Meyer. eds. 1995. *The Verb in Contemporary English*. Cambridge: Cambridge University Press.
Aitchison, J. 1991. *Language Change: Progress or Decay?* Cambridge: Cambridge University Press.
**American Heritage Dictionary of the English Language*. 1992. Boston: Houghton.
Archangeli, D. and D. T. Langendoen. eds. 1997. *Optimality Theory: An Overview*. Malden, MA and Oxford: Blackwell.
Arnold, J. et al. eds. 1996. *Sociolinguistic Variation: Data, Theory, and Analysis*. Stanford: Center for the Study of Language and Information.
Ball, C. N. 1996. "A Diachronic Study of Relative Markers in Spoken and Written English." *Language Variation and Change* Vol. 8. pp. 227-58.
Barber, C. 1993. *The English Language*. Cambridge: Cambridge University Press.
Bauer, L. 1983. *English Word-Formation*. Cambridge: Cambridge University Press.
―――. 1994. *Watching English Change*. London and New York: Longman.
Beard, H. and C. Cerf. 1993. *The Official Politically Correct Dictionary and Handbook*. New York: Villard Books.
Bebout, L. 1984. "Asymmetries in Male-Female Word Pairs." *American Speech* Vol. 59. pp. 13-30.
Biber, D. et al. 1999. *Longman Grammar of Spoken and Written English*. London: Longman.
Blake, N. ed. 1992. *The Cambridge History of the English Language Vol. II:*

1066-1476. Cambridge: Cambridge University Press.

Blyth, C., S. Recktenwald and J. Wang. 1990. "I'm Like, 'Say What?!': A New Quotative in American Oral Narrative." *American Speech* Vol. 65. pp. 215-27.

Burchfield, R. W. ed. 1996. *The New Fowler's Modern English Usage*. Oxford: Oxford University Press.

Butters, R. R. 1980. "Narrative Go 'Say'." *American Speech* Vol. 55. pp. 304-7.

Campbell, L. 1998. *Historical Linguistics*. Edinburgh: Edinburgh University Press.

Cannon, G. 1987. *Historical Change and English Word-Formation: Recent Vocabulary*. New York: Peter Lang.

Carr, P. 1993. *Phonology*. London: Macmillan.

千葉修司. 1995. 「補文標識 that の消去 － That 消去の現象の記述を中心に－」『津田塾大学紀要』第 27 号 pp. 1-44.

Coates, J. 1986. *Women, Men and Language*. London: Longman.

Collins, C. 1991. "Why and How Come." *MIT Working Papers in Linguistics* 15. ed. by L. Cheng. and H. Demirdache. pp. 31-45.

Courtenay, Edward S. C. 1855. *Courtenay's Dictionary of Abbreviations*. London: Groombridge & Sons.

Coye, D. 1994. "A Linguistic Survey of College Freshmen: Keeping Up with Standard American English." *American Speech* Vol. 69. pp. 260-284.

Crystal, D. 1997. *English as a Global Language*. Cambrigde: Cambridge University Press.

Culicover, P. W. 1976. *Syntax*. New York: Academic Press.

_____. 1997. *Principles and Parameters*. Oxford: Oxford University Press.

Culpeper, J. 1997. *History of English*. London and New York: Routledge.

Denison, D. 1993. *English Historical Syntax*. London and New York: Longman.

_____. 1998. "Syntax." *The Cambridge History of the English Language. Vol. IV: 1776-1997*. ed. by S. Romaine. pp. 92-329. Cambrigde: Cambridge University Press.

Dixon, R. M. W. 1991. *A New Approach to English Grammar on Semantic Principles*. Oxford: Oxford University Press.

Dresher, B. E. 1999. "Charting the Learning Path: Cues to Parameter Setting." *Linguistic Inquiry* 30. pp. 27-67.

Ferrara, K. and B. Bell. 1995. "Sociolinguistic Variation and Discourse Function of Constructed Dialogue Introducers: The Case of *be+like*." *American Speech* Vol. 70. pp. 265-290.

Fowler, H. W. 1965². *A Dictionary of Modern English Usage*. Oxford: Clarendon Press.

Freidin, R. ed. 1991. *Principles and Parameters in Comparative Grammar*. Cambridge, Mass.: MIT Press.

福地肇. 1995. 『英語らしい表現と英文法』研究社

Fukui, N. 1986. "Leftward Spread: Compensatory Lengthening and Gemination in Japanese." *Linguistic Inquiry* 17. pp. 359-64.

Givón, T. 1993. *English Grammar: A Function-Based Introduction*. 2 vols. Amsterdam: John Benjamins.

Guy, G. R. and R. Bayley. 1995. "On the Choice of Relative Forms in English." *American Speech* Vol. 95. pp. 148-162.

Guy, G. R. et al. eds. 1996. *Towards a Social Science of Language. Vol. 1. Variation and Change in Language and Society*. Amsterdam and Philadelphia: John Benjamins.

Haegeman, L. and J. Guéron. 1999. *English Grammar: A Generative Perspective*. Oxford: Blackwell.

Hammond, M. 1997. "Optimality Theory and Prosody." *Optimality Theory*. ed. by D. Archangeli. and D. T. Langendoen. pp. 33-58.

―――. 1997. "Vowel Quantity and Syllabification in English." *Language* Vol. 73. pp. 1-17.

Hattori, N. 1991. *Mechanisms of Word Accent Change: Innovations in Standard Japanese*. Tokyo: Shinozaki Shorin.

―――. 1998. "Base Transparency in Suprasegmental Changes: Ongoing

Changes in Japanese and English." *Language Variation and Change* Vol. 10. pp. 85-96.

堀井令以知. 1990. 『女の言葉』明治書院

Hornby, A. S. 1975². *Guide to Patterns and Usage in English*. London: Oxford University Press.

Hornstein, N. and D. Lightfoot. 1991. "On the Nature of Lexical Government." *Principles and Parameters in Comparative Grammar*. ed. by R. Freidin. pp. 365-91.

Huddleston, R. D. 1984. *Introduction to the Grammar of English*. Cambridge: Cambridge University Press.

Hughes, A. and P. Trudgill. 1979. *English Accents and Dialects*. London: Edward Arnold.

今西典子・浅野一郎 1990. 『照応と削除』大修館書店

Inada, T. and N. Imanishi. 1997. "Complement Selection and Inversion in Embedded Clauses." *Studies in English Linguistics*. ed. by M. Ukaji. et al. pp. 345-77. Tokyo: Taishukan Publishing.

Jespersen, O. 1909-49. *A Modern English Grammar on Historical Principles*. 7 vols. London and Copenhagen: Allen & Unwin, and Munksgaard.

Kajita, M. 1977. "Towards a Dynamic Model of Syntax." *Studies in English Linguistics* Vol. 5. pp. 41-76.

Kay, P. 1984. "The *Kind of/Sort of* Construction." *BLS* Vol. 10. pp. 157-71.

Kennedy, A. G. 1933. "The Future of the English Language." *American Speech* Vol. 4. pp. 3-12.

Labov, W. 1994. *Principles of Linguistic Change I: Internal Factors*. Oxford: Blackwell

―――. 1996. "When Intuitions Fail." *CLS* Vol. 32. pp. 77-105.

Laver, J. 1981. "Linguistic Routines and Politeness in Greeting and Parting." *Conversational Routine*. ed. by F. Coulmas. The Hague: Mouton.

Levin, B. 1993. *English Verb Classes and Alternations*. Chicago and London: the University of Chicago Press.

Lightfoot, D. 1999. *The Development of Language*. Oxford: Blackwell.

Maggio, R. 1991. *The Dictionary of Bias-Free Usage*. Arizona: Oryx.

McDavid, V. 1964. "The Alternation of *That* and Zero in Noun Clauses." *American Speech* Vol. 39. pp. 102-13.

Milroy, J. 1992. *Linguistic Variation and Change*. Oxford: Blackwell.

———— and L. Milroy. 1999³. *Authority in Language: Investigating Standard English*. London and New York: Routledge.

Moravcsik, E. A. 1978. "Agreements." *Universals of Human Language: Syntax*. ed. by J. H. Greenberg. Vol. 4. pp. 331-74. Stanford, CA : Stanford University Press.

Morris, W. and M. 1975. *Harper Dictionary of Contemporary Usage*. London: Harper and Row.

*OED : *The Oxford English Dictionary*. 1989². Oxford : Clarendon Press.

Osselton, N. E. 1982. "On the Use of the Perfect in Present-Tense Narrative." *English Studies* Vol. 63. pp. 63-9.

Quirk, R. et al. 1985. *A Comprehensive Grammar of the English Language*. London and New York: Longman.

*Random House: *The Random House Dictionary of the English Language*. 1987². New York: Random House.

Rickford, J. R. and T. A. Wasow. 1995. "Syntactic Variation and Change in Progress: Loss of the Verbal Coda in Topic-Restricting *As Far As* Constructions." *Language* Vol. 71. pp. 102-31.

Romaine, S. 1994. *Language in Society: An Introduction to Sociolinguistics*. Oxford: Oxford University Press.

———— and D. Lange. 1991. "The Use of *Like* as a Marker of Reported Speech and Thought: A Case of Grammaticalization in Progress." *American Speech* Vol. 66. pp. 227-79.

Sapir, E. 1921. *Language*. New York: Harcourt.

Schneider, E. W. 1996. "Constraints on the Loss of Case Marking in English *Wh*-Pronouns: Four Hundred Year of Real-Time Evidence." *Sociolinguistic*

Variation. ed. by J. Arnold. et al. pp. 487-99.

*SOD: *The New Shorter Oxford English Dictionary*. 1993. Oxford: Clarendon Press.

Tabor, W. 1993. "The Gradual Development of Degree Modifier *Sort of* and *Kind of*: A Corpus Proximity Model." *CLS* Vol. 29. pp. 451-65.

Thompson, S. A. and A. Mulac. 1991. "The Discourse Conditions for the Use of Complementizer *That* in Conversational English." *Journal of Pragmatics* Vol. 15. pp. 237-51.

Trask, R. L. 1996. *Historical Linguistics*. London: Arnold.

Trudgill, P. ed. 1984. *Language in the British Isles*. Cambridge: Cambridge University Press.

———— and J. Hannah. 1985^2. 1994^3. *International English*. London: Arnold.

Tysell, H. T. 1935. "The English of the Comic Cartoons." *American Speech* Vol. 10. pp. 43-55.

Underhill, R. 1976. *Turkish Grammar*. Cambridge, Mass.: MIT Press.

————. 1988. "*Like* is, Like, Focus." *American Speech* Vol. 63. pp. 234-46.

U. S. Department of Labor. 1977. *Dictionary of Occupational Titles*. Washington, D. C.: U. S. Government Printing Office.

*Webster: *Webster's Third New International Dictionary*. 1961. London: Bell.

Wells, J. 1982. *Accents of English*. Cambridge: Cambridge University Press.

———— 1990. *Longman Pronunciation Dictionary*. London: Longman.

Wolfram, W. and N. Schilling-Estes. 1998. *American English: Dialects and Variation*. Malden, MA and Oxford: Blackwell.

事　項　索　引

あ(行)

アクセント
　　～の揺れ　146-151
アクロニム(acronym)　94, 127-128
上げ→母音
一致　95-98
　　(either) A or B と動詞の～　96
　　neither A nor B と動詞の～　96-97
　　(n)either と動詞の～　96
　　none と動詞の～　95-96
　　there 構文の～　96
　　this/that と kind(sort)の～　98
　　what 節の～　96
　　集合名詞と動詞の～　95
　　主語と動詞の～　95-97
意味変化
　　語彙の～　129
隠語(argot)　112
受身　62-64, 68, 182
　　間接目的語の～　62-63
婉曲(euphemism)　157, 163-166
男ことば　159-161
音交替　136
音節境界　138
音節脱落　143-144
オンセット(onset)　143
女ことば　159-161

か(行)

外置
　　NP からの～　85
外来起源語　115
格
　　～接辞　108
過去形　57-58, 103-104, 183
　　～と現在完了　57-58
　　規則形　103-104
　　原形と同形の～　104
過去分詞　31-33, 40, 103-104
数えられる名詞→名詞/可算名詞
仮定法　64-67, 83
　　it is time につづく～　66
関係詞→(関係)代名詞
関係節

再叙代名詞(resumptive pronoun)　26
制限用法　22, 24-25
　　ゼロ～　20-22
　　代名詞を先行詞とする～　27
　　二重制限の～(double relative)　25
非制限用法　22, 24-25, 27
　　that-～　20-22
　　wh-～　20-22
冠詞　29-30
　　～の交替　29
　　～の省略　93-94
　　不定～　6-7
間接話法　19
感嘆文　183
間投詞(interjection)　160
完了　57-58
　　現在完了　57-58, 183
　　～と過去形　57-58
　　過去時の副詞と共起する～　58
　　be＋過去分詞の～　58
規則動詞化　183
規則変化　103-104
基体(base)　115, 146
機能語　133
疑問文
　　多重～(multiple question)　20
逆形成(back formation)　122
強意語(intensifier)　168
強勢　146-151
　　無強勢音節　133, 137, 142-143
共鳴音(sonorant)　143
空所化(gapping)　81
　　擬似～(pseudo-gapping)　82
屈折　124
　　～接辞　107
クリオール　179
形容詞
　　限定用法(attributive)　32-33, 104
　　　　a-形容詞の～　33
　　叙述用法(predicative)　32, 104, 113
　　節を従える～　31-32
　　a-～　33
　　-y に終わる～　102-103
形容詞化
　　過去分詞の～　32-33
　　名詞の～　32

結果を表す表現　74
結合形(combining form)　120
　　接頭辞的～　120-121
　　接尾辞的～　121
懸垂分詞(dangling participle)　183
限定用法→形容詞
語彙　105-129
語彙化(lexicalize)　123
語彙拡散(lexical diffusion)　4
拘束形　107
声
　　～の揺れ　132-133
呼応　5, 97-98
　　everyone/anybodyの～　97
　　oneの～　97
コーダ(coda)　143
語境界　135
語形　101-104
　　形容詞・副詞の～　102-103
　　動詞の～　103-104
　　名詞の～　101-102
語形成　105
語順　99-100, 156
語中境界　135
混交(contamination)　33
混成(portmanteau)　129

さ(行)

最上級　102-103
　　絶対最上級(absolute superative)　33
　　副詞の～　30
削除→省略
下げ→母音
差別語　153-156
　　語順の問題　156
　　代名詞の問題　156
　　男性中心語(androcentric)　156
子音　132-136
　　～の音交替　136
　　～の削除　133-134
　　～の挿入　134-135
　　～の母音化　135, 140
歯茎音　143
　　後部～(postalveolar)　140
辞書項目　107
時制　57-60
実際の時間軸(real time)　3, 102, 150
史的現在　58
史的流れ(drift)　4
自動詞　67-77

自動詞化　68-69, 75-77
　　前置詞添加による～　76
　　NP削除による～　75-76
　　self削除による～　76
借入　105-112
　　～語　107-111
　　日本語～　110
　　翻訳～　111
自由形　107
重子音化　3
従節＋主節の構文(periodic sentence)
　　～の照応　98
主節＋従節の構文(loose sentence)
　　～の照応　98
主要部(head)　8, 11, 123, 124
照応(anaphora)　97-98
　　従節＋主節における～　97-98
　　主節＋従節における～　98
称号(title)　173-176
　　結婚と～　174
　　Ms　155
小範疇語　107
省略　79-94, 183
　　冠詞の～　93-94
　　助動詞の～　82
　　接続詞の～　83-88
　　　　関係副詞thatの省略　85
　　　　andの省略　87
　　　　asの省略　87-88
　　　　ifの省略　88
　　　　thatの省略　83-87
　　前置詞の～　88-93
　　　　NP修飾の不定詞における～　90-91
　　代名詞の～　79-81
　　　　Iの省略　80
　　　　itの省略　79-80
　　　　youの省略　80
　　直接目的語の～　81
　　動詞の～　81-82
　　　　空所化(gapping)　81
　　名詞の～　79-81
　　thatの～　65
　　whatの～　80
叙述用法→形容詞
女性語　157-159
助動詞
　　～と否定　36-37
助動詞削除　82
所有格→格/属格
唇音(labial)　134, 143
進行形　60-62, 182

数量詞
　　〜と否定　37
姓　155
性(gender)　11-12,108
性差(sexism)　117,153-161
生産的(productive)　106-108,115-116,120
政治的公正(political correctness, PC)　164-165
声門閉鎖音化(glottalization)　135
節
　　同格〜　84
　　内容〜　68
　　it that〜　69
　　that〜　68-73
　　what〜　96
接辞
　　〜添加(affixation)　105
　　屈折〜　107
　　時制〜　183
　　所有格〜　183
　　接頭辞(prefix)　75,119-120,122,148
　　　　〜削除　122
　　　　〜による他動詞化　75
　　接尾辞(suffix)　116-119
　　　　形容詞を形成する〜　117-118,148
　　　　動詞を形成する〜　118
　　　　副詞を形成する〜　118-119
　　　　名詞を形成する〜　116-117
　　代名詞の格〜　183
　　派生〜　107,115-122
　　比較の〜　183
　　複数〜　183
接続詞　55-56
　　〜の省略　83-88
　　〜の副詞化　42-43
舌頂音(coronal)　134
接頭辞→接辞
接尾辞→接辞
切離構造(tmesis)　127
前置詞　47-53
　　〜化
　　　　形容詞(句)の〜　52
　　　　接続詞の〜　51
　　〜の交替　47-49
　　〜の残留(p-stranding)　19,23,49-50
　　〜の省略　88-93
　　〜の添加　76
　　二重〜構文　50-51
前置詞句
　　〜からの取り出し　49-50
　　場所をあらわす〜　99
造語　111-112

新造語(neologism)　105
促音化　3
属格(所有格)　8-11
　　群〜(group genitive)　11
　　主格〜　9
　　同格〜　9
　　二重〜　10
　　部分的〜　9
　　目的格〜　9

た(行)

代不定詞
　　〜to の省略　92
代名詞　97-98,156
　　2人称〜　171-172
　　関係〜(relative pronoun)　20-27
　　疑問〜　18-20
　　再叙〜(resumptive pronoun)　26
　　指示〜　18
　　〜の性　11,12
　　人称〜　15-16
　　不定〜　16,17,95-96
多音節語　184
脱落　131
他動詞　67-77
他動詞化　68-75,182
　　接頭辞による〜　75
　　前置詞省略による〜　71-72
　　it の添加による〜　69
タブー(taboo)　160,163,167,184
　　宗教的〜　165
単音節語　103,137,139,184
短化(abbreviation)　105-106,112,127-128
短化→母音
男性語　157-159
　　男性中心語(androcentric)　156
断定的述語(assertive predicate)　87
単複同形　101
誓い(swearing)　160,167-169
　　漫画の〜　169
中間動詞(middle verb)　67-68,76-77
中性化　153-154
長化→母音
直説法　64-67
　　〜現在　65
直接話法　19
綴字発音　144-145
丁重さ(politeness)　160,170-172
転換　105,112-115
　　A＞N の〜　112-113

A＞Vの〜　115
　　Adv＞Nの〜　115
　　N＞Aの〜　113
　　N＞Vの〜　113-114
　　V＞Nの〜　114-115
　　verb＋particle＞Nの〜　112
伝達動詞　58
統一性原理(uniformity principle)　4
同化　131
同格節　84
動詞・副詞結合(V-Adv)　29,182
動詞化　113
動詞句(VP)削除　82
倒置　99-100
　　従節の〜　99-100
倒置条件(inverted condition)　67
透明(endocentric)　123
　　不透明(exocentric)　123
動名詞　183

な(行)

名前　173-176
　　姓(last name)　173-176
　　名(first name)　173-176
軟口蓋音(velar)　134,140
二重前置詞構文　50-51
能格動詞(ergative verb)　67-68,76-77
のろい(expletive)　167

は(行)

倍数　51-52
歯擦音
　　歯茎〜　143
派生(derivation)　112,115-122
　　ゼロ〜　106,183
　　動詞からの〜(deverbal)　124
　　〜接辞　107,115-122
発話様態動詞(manner-of-speaking verb)　85
罵倒(ばとう)　167-169
　　〜語　158
比較　33
　　絶対比較級(absolute comparative)　33
　　比較級　102-103
ピジン　179
非断定的述語(non-assertive predicate)　87
否定　35-39
　　〜の scope　36-38
　　助動詞と〜　36-37
　　準動詞(verbal)の〜　35

　　数量詞と〜　37
　　多重〜　39
鼻母音　109
ファーストネーム→名前
フォルマント　139
付加詞(adjunct)　49
不規則動詞　183
複合(compounding)　105,112,122-127
複合形容詞→形容詞複合語
複合語　103-104,122-127,146
　　形容詞〜　125-126
　　語根〜(root compound)　124
　　総合的〜(synthetic compound)　124
　　動詞〜　126
　　名詞〜　124-125
複合動詞→動詞複合語
複合名詞→名詞複合語
副詞　35-46
　　強調詞(intensifier)　40-41
　　否定の　〜99
　　文〜　39,41
　　平坦〜(flat adverb)　39
　　様態副詞　41
　　-ly　149
副詞化　42-44
　　形容詞＋前置詞の〜　43
　　接続詞の〜　42-43
　　前置詞の〜　43
複数
　　〜接辞　108
複数形　5,6,101-102,108
　　規則〜　101-102
　　単複同形　101
　　不規則〜　101-102
　　分節的〜　5
不定詞　90,183
不透明(exocentric)　123
分詞構文　183
分数　51-52
文副詞　41
文法化　60
文法形態素　107
文法語　107
分裂文(cleft sentence)　26,84
　　擬似〜(pseudo cleft sentence)　68
閉鎖音
　　声門〜　135
　　無声〜　140
　　有声〜　140
平叙文　183
変異(variant, linguistic variable)　2

変移動詞(mutative verb) 58
母音 136-144
　2重母音 143
　2重母音化 132,136-137,139-141,182
　交替 103
　持続変化 136-138
　　短化 136-138
　　長化 136-138
　垂直変化 136,139-140
　　上げ 139-140
　　下げ 140
　水平変化 136,138-139
　　後舌化 139
　　前舌化 138-139
　単音化 136,141-142
　中舌化 142-143
　鼻母音 109
　〜の脱落(aphaeresis) 143
ぼかし表現(hedge, approximator) 45-46,159-160
補部(complement) 49
補文(complement clause) 86,99,183
補文標識(complementizer)
　〜for 92
本来起源語 115

ま(行)

摩擦音
　前方〜(anterior fricative) 140
見掛け時間(apparent time) 3
無強勢音節 133,137,142,143
無標 61,157
名詞
　〜の形容詞用法 5
　可算〜 7
　固有〜 128
　集合〜 95
　派生〜 13,114
　不可算〜 6

名詞化
　形容詞の〜 14
　代名詞の〜 16
　動詞・副詞結合(V-Adv)の〜 29
　副詞の〜 13
　普通〜 6-7
命令文 183
モデル 13,146

や・ら・わ(行)

4文字語(four-letter word) 106,163-164
有標(marked) 38
ら抜きことば 3
リアルタイム→実際の時間軸
類型変化(typological change) 4
話題化 80
割れ(breaking) 139,140

be like 構文 59-60
Belfast English 100
blend(ing) 105-106
blocking 115
floating 17
head-final 123
head-initial 123
light verb 108
P-stranding→前置詞
Particle 112,124-126
PC→政治的公正
pied-piping 19,23
rhotic→rを発音する
RP 135-136,141
rを発音する(rhotic) 135-136
there 構文 96
V-final 言語 116
V-initial 言語 116
V-medial 言語 116

語句索引

a 29
a couple(of) 92
a lot 40
a variety(of) 92
-able 117-118,148
absent(from) 91
according(to) 91
-al 116
all 6
alongside 45
alongside(of) 92
alot 17
already 38
also 38
among 53
and
　　〜の省略 87
answer yes(no) 44
any 39
anybody
　　〜の呼応 97
anymore 44
approaching 44
-ary 148
as
　　〜の省略 87-88
as…as
　　譲歩の〜 56
as far as 51
　　as far as…(be concerned) 82
　　(as)far as…be concerned 87
at all 38-39
-ative 148
back of 52
before 52
behind 52
between 53
both 30
busy(busily)-ing 46
(by)way of 92
come it 69
coupla(＜a couple of) 60,92
damn(ed) 40,168
de- 120
dis- 120
-dom 117

don't(didn't)not… 39
due(to) 52,91
each 17
each other 17
-ee 117
either 96
-en
　　形容詞を形成する〜 118
　　動詞を形成する〜 118
…enough that(＝so…that) 44
-er 102-103,116-117
-ese 117
-ess 154,117
-est 102-103
-ette 117
even as 45
every which way 27
everyone
　　〜の呼応 97
except
　　unless の意の〜 56
for as long as 56
(for)sake of 92
fucking 41
-ful 116
girl 154
go it 69
granted 43
heck 168
hell 41,168
home 44
how about 19-20
how come 19
how long since… 44
however 42
-ic 116
if
　　〜の省略 88
　　whether の意の〜 55
(in)back of 92
in front of 52
inside(of) 92
(in)spite of 92
ir- 120
-ish 116,117
-ism 117

索引　203

-ist　116-117
it　42
　　～の省略　79-80
　　it that　68-69
　　非人称主語の～　79
it is time(that)...　66
its　27
It's me　15,182
-ity　115-116
-ize　118
just in case　42-43
kind
　　this/that と～の一致　98
kind of　46
lady　154
-less　116
like　45
　　接続詞の～　56
　　be like 構文　59-60
liketa(<like to)　60
live it　69
-ly　116,118,149
-man　154,156
-master　154
mid-　120
-mistress　154
momentarily　45
more　102-103
most　102-103
Ms　155
much　40
myself　15
near(to)　92
neither　96-97
-ness　115-116
never　35-36
no　36,171
no matter that　56
non-　119
none　95-96
not　35
not as... as　33,38
noway　46
of　8-11
(of) course　92
of which　23-24
on account of　56
one　16-17
　　～の呼応　97
one another　17
one day　45

-ous　116
outside(of)　92
over-　120
place　44
plenty　41
presently　45
pretty　40
re-　119
regardless(of)　91
right　41
-s　108
's　8-11
-self
　　～削除による自動詞化　76
short of　52
so　42
so...(that)　84
soon's＜as soon as　87
sort
　　this/that と～の一致　98
sort of　46
sufficiently...that(＝so...that)　44
suposeta(＜supposed to)　60
that
　　～節　68-73
　　～の省略　83-87
　　関係詞の～　20-22,24-26
　　指示代名詞の～　18
　　that...that(＝so...that)　43-44
　　副詞の～　43-44
that's　24,27
the　29-30
　　～と副詞の最上級　30
　　～の省略　93-94
　　～と both　30
the reason is because　55-56
there　45
　　～構文　96
this
　　副詞の～　43
　　指示代名詞の～　18,88
thou　172
though　42
till　52
time　44
to　52
too　38,46
un-　119
under-　120
until　52
very　40

-ward 119
was
　～/were の選択　67
way　93
well　45
were
　was/～の選択　67
what
　～節　96
whether　55
which　24-27

who　1,18-19,23-26
whom　1,18,23
whose　23-24,27
why don't you　19
-wise　118
woman　154
-woman　154,156
-y　102-103,116,118
yes　36,171
yet　38

あとがき

　本書の著者、中尾俊夫先生は英語の歴史に関する著作、特に音韻史に関する数多くの業績を残されて2000年5月にご逝去なさいました。本書はその先生が闘病を続ける中で精力的に執筆を進められて、ついには絶筆となったご遺稿を整理、編集したものです。

　本書の構想——21世紀の英語がどのような方向に進んでいくのか——は実質的には1995年夏に開かれた津田塾セミナーの講演から始められました。その執筆にあたり先生は現在人気を博している英米の作家の小説を読まれ、その数は130冊を優に超えています(本書に引用されている例はすべてこれらの作品からご自身で集められたものです)。

　先生は、その長く厳しい研究生活の中で、絶えず「変化はなぜ起こるのか」「何が変わって、何が変わらないのか」さらには、「どのように変わるのか」など、その原因とメカニズムの解明に取り組まれておられました。そして最終的には、さまざまな言語の通時的普遍、すなわち多くの言語によって共有され、繰り返される、無標の史的変化は何か、それらを統御する一般原則は何かを明らかにしようとされていました。

　ご遺稿はルーズリーフで200枚ほどの手書きメモの形で、決して完全原稿と呼べるものではありませんでした(例えば、第一章などはお亡くなりになる直前にお書きになったもので、最後にはお書きになることがかなわず、口述筆記やテープ録音した箇所もあり、もう少し時間があれば...、という感を抱かせる章となっています)。その中には、データだけ整理してあって、その分析・記述については考察中であるとか、それとは逆に、項目の記述だけできていて関連するデータが集められていないという箇所もありました。ご

遺稿の編集を任された私どもの力量不足もあって、完成までに思わぬ月日が費やされてしまいましたが、編集の際に特に配慮したことは、できるだけご遺稿の原形をくずさないようにするということと、資料の正確さという2点にあります。前者については、文体などに手を入れることによって少しでも説明の記述がわかりやすくなるように努めました。後者については、引用例は極力原典にあたって、チェックを行ないました (どうしてもチェックできず、不本意ながら削除した例や、やむを得ず作家名のみ挙げて、例をそのまま残した箇所もあります)。

　本書を完成するにあたって、多くの方々のご援助をいただきました。2章から12章まで(統語論)については津田塾大学の千葉修司氏、池内正幸氏、東京大学の今西典子氏、13-14章(形態論)は茨城大学の竝木崇康氏、15章(音韻論)は筑波大学の山田宣夫氏、16-20章(社会言語学)は三重大学の服部範子氏にそれぞれお力添えをいただきました。厚くお礼申し上げます。

　先生のご遺志は本書を、英語を専攻する大学生向けの英語学・英文法・社会言語学の教科書として出版するというものでした。この趣旨にご賛同をいただきましたひつじ書房の松本功氏、編集作業でお世話になりました郷野伊都代さんには心よりお礼を申し上げます。

2003年3月　　　　　　　　　　　　　　　　　　　　　　　　児馬　修
　　　　　　　　　　　　　　　　　　　　　　　　　　　　　寺島　廸子

〔著者〕　**中尾俊夫**　……………………………　なかお　としお　…………………

〔略歴〕　1934年　横浜生まれ
　　　　1958-61年　東京教育大学大学院博士課程在学
　　　　1985-86年　ダラム大学招聘特別研究員（Sidney Holgate Fellow）
　　　　元津田塾大学教授。文学博士

〔著書〕　『英語史Ⅱ（中英語）』（大修館書店 1972）、The Prosodic Phonology of Late Middle English（Shinozaki 1978）、『英語発達史』（篠崎書林　1979）、『英語史Ⅰ（古英語）』（共著）（大修館書店 1980）、『音韻史』（大修館書店　1985）、Historical Studies in Honor of Taizo Hirose (ed.) (Kenkyusha 1987)、『図説英語史入門』（共著）（大修館書店　1988）、『英語の歴史』（講談社 1989）、『歴史的にさぐる現代の英文法』（共編著）（大修館書店 1990）、『音韻における通時的普遍』（リーベル出版　1996）、『社会言語学概論』（共著）（くろしお出版　1997）など。

〔編者〕　東京学芸大学教授　児馬修
　　　　滋賀県立大学教授　寺島廸子

変化する英語

発行　　　　2003年7月7日

定価	1600円＋税
著者	©中尾俊夫
発行者	松本功
装丁者	盛早苗 (ae)
印刷所・製本所	三美印刷 株式会社
発行所	有限会社 ひつじ書房

〒112-0002　文京区小石川 5-21-5
Tel 03-5684-6871　Fax 03-5684-6872
郵便振替　00120-8-142852
toiawase@hituzi.co.jp
http://www.hituzi.co.jp

造本には充分注意しておりますが、落丁・乱丁などがございましたら、小社またはお買い上げ書店にておとりかえいたします。
ご意見・ご感想など、小社までお寄せくだされば幸いです。

◆

ISBN4-89476-188-2 C1082
Printed in Japan

日本語研究叢書刊行案内

第1期
- ◎1-1　日本語動詞の諸相　村木新次郎著　4000円
- ◎1-2　改訂版　古代日本語動詞のテンス・アスペクト——源氏物語の分析——　鈴木泰著　5000円
- ◎1-3　現代日本語の語構成論研究——語における形と意味——　斎藤倫明著　4700円
- ◎1-4　日本語のモダリティと人称　仁田義雄著　3200円
- ◎1-5　視点と主観性——日英語助動詞の分析——　澤田治美著　4400円

第2期
- ◎2-1　認知文法論　山梨正明著　4200円
- ◎2-2　日本語の引用　鎌田修著　3200円
- 　2-3　日本語の存在表現の歴史　金水敏著
- ◎2-4　文法と語形成　影山太郎著　4854円
- 　2-5　言語運用と言語事実　アンドレイ・ベケシュ著
- 　2-6　日本語における談話の管理について　田窪行則著
- ◎2-7　アスペクト・テンス体系とテクスト　工藤真由美著　4200円
- ◎2-8　日本語形態論　城田俊著　4000円

第3期
- ◎3-1　日本語のテクスト——関係・効果・様相——　野村眞木夫著　4800円
- 　3-2　日本語名詞句の意味論と語用論　西山佑司著　4800円　2003年秋刊行！
- 　3-3　未定（「引用」に関するもの）藤田保幸著
- 　3-4　言語行動という視点　杉戸清樹著
- 　3-5　奄美大島（北部）方言の文法　石崎公曹・松本泰丈共著
- 　3-6　言語接触と言語変容——日系二世カナダ人の日英語における変異——　日比谷潤子著

◎＋ゴシックのものは既刊。表示の値段は税抜価格です。その時点での消費税が加算されます。『言語』には毎月、広告をだしておりますので、ご覧ください。また、最新の情報はひつじ書房のホームページに掲載しています。http://www.hituzi.co.jp/をご覧ください。

日本語研究資料集刊行案内

第1期　編集代表　加藤泰彦・工藤浩・鈴木泰・仁田義雄・村木新次郎

●第1期刊行書目・編集担当者●

1-1	モダリティ	仁田義雄・益岡隆志
1-2, 3	テンス・アスペクト	鈴木泰・澤田治美・工藤真由美・森山卓郎
1-4	ヴォイス	村木新次郎・外池滋生
1-5	否定	加藤泰彦・井上優
1-6	活用	村木新次郎・屋名池誠
◎**1-7**	指示詞	金水敏・田窪行則　2500円
◎**1-8**	動詞の自他	須賀一好・早津恵美子　2700円
1-9	はとが	上林洋二・丹羽哲也
1-10	格	仁田義雄・小矢野哲夫
1-11	とりたて	野田尚史・沼田善子
1-12	副詞	工藤浩・矢澤真人
◎**1-13**	語構成	斎藤倫明・石井正彦　3100円
1-14	語の意味	山田進・相澤正夫

★巻数が、ゴシック+◎のものは既刊。『指示詞』は重版予定です。
★表示の値段は税抜価格。2500円から3500円のあいだです。
★『言語』には毎月、広告をだしておりますので、ご覧ください。
★上記の情報は、2003年7月現在のものです。
★また、最新の情報はひつじ書房のホームページに掲載しています。
　http://www.hituzi.co.jp/をご覧ください。

ひつじ研究叢書（言語編）

- 第 1 巻　方言地理学の展開
  　　　　徳川宗賢著　　　15000 円
- 　第 2 巻　中古中世の言葉遣いの研究
  　　　　森野宗明著　予15000 円
- 第 4 巻　古代日本語母音論
  　　　―上代特殊仮名遣の再解釈―
  　　　　松本克己著　　　9000 円
- 第 5 巻　バントゥ諸語
  　　　　動詞アクセントの研究
  　　　　湯川恭敏著　　　19000 円
- 第 6 巻　Studies in English and Japanese Auxiliaries
  　　　　: A Multi-stratal Approach
  　　　　澤田治美著　　　12000 円
- 第 7 巻　言語の時間表現（重版予定）
  　　　　金子亨著
- 第 8 巻　拾遺　日本文法論
  　　　　奥津敬一郎著　　5825 円
- 第 9 巻　日本語条件表現史の研究
  　　　　小林賢次著　　　12000 円
- 第10巻　束縛関係
  　　　　中村捷著　　　　6019 円
- 第11巻　意味分析の方法　―理論と実践―
  　　　　森田良行著　　　3800 円
- 第12巻　上代語の構文と表記
  　　　　佐佐木隆著　　　14000 円
- 第13巻　日本語文法の諸問題
  　　　―高橋太郎先生古希記念論文集―
  　　　　鈴木泰・角田太作編　4200 円
- 第14巻　日本語文法　―体系と方法―
  　　　　川端善明・仁田義雄編　10000 円
- 第15巻　日本語方言一型アクセントの研究
  　　　　山口幸洋著　　　19000 円
- 第16巻　複合動詞の構造と意味用法
  　　　　姫野昌子著　　　6000 円
- 第17巻　現代言語理論と格
  　　　　石綿敏雄著　　　4600 円
- 第18巻　萬葉集と上代語
  　　　　佐佐木隆著　　　22000 円
- 第19巻　日本語記述文法の理論
  　　　　近藤泰弘著　　　19000 円
- 第20巻　日英語の自他の交替
  　　　　丸田忠雄・須賀一好編　5000 円
- 第21巻　日本語　意味と文法の風景
  　　　―国広哲弥教授古稀記念論文集―
  　　　　山田進・菊地康人・籾山洋介編　6000 円
- 第22巻　日本語の情報構造と統語構造
  　　　　カレル・フィアラ著　28000 円
- 第23巻　Old English Constructions with Multiple Predicates
  　　　　大門正幸著　　　7400 円
- 第24巻　Bound variables and coreferential pronouns : Zero and overt pronouns in Japanese and English
  　　　　杉浦滋子著　　　13000 円
- 第25巻　日本語モダリティの史的研究
  　　　　高山善行著　　　12000 円
- 第26巻　Discourse Politeness in Japanese Conversation
  　　　　宇佐美まゆみ著　6560 円
- 第27巻　日本語文法の発想
  　　　　森田良行著　　　3200 円
- 第28巻　文法化とイディオム化
  　　　　秋元実治著　　　3600 円
- 第29巻　日本語修飾構造の語用論的研究
  　　　　加藤重広著　　　8000 円
- 　第30巻　語彙論的語構成論
  　　　　斎藤倫明著　　　5200 円
- 　第31巻　現代日本語の漢語動名詞の研究
  　　　　小林英樹著　　　6000 円
- 　第32巻　方言学的日本史の方法
  　　　　小林隆著　　　　18400 円

○は既刊のもの（2003年7月現在）。

★表示の価格は税抜価格です。その時点での消費税が加算されます。

★『言語』には毎月、広告をだしておりますので、ご覧ください。また、最新の情報はひつじ書房のホームページに掲載しています。
　こちら（http://www.hituzi.co.jp/）をご覧ください。

2003-7-G

ひつじ研究叢書（言語教育編）

第1巻　日本語複合動詞の習得研究　松田文子著　7000円
　　2004年春刊行予定
　　第二言語習得において複合動詞は文法形式と語彙の両面の要素を持ち、極めて重要な役割を果たしている。本書では複合動詞「〜こむ」を事例として取り上げ、意味およびその習得と語彙習得支援に関し考察を行う。

第2巻　統語構造を中心とした日本語とタイ語の対照研究
　　　　田中寛著　19000円
　　2004年春刊行予定
　　タイ語研究、および日本語との対照研究の諸問題を明らかにする。本書は、科研費助成基盤研究報告を修訂し再検討したものである。研究の成果・方法論はタイ語をはじめとする東南アジア諸語の言語学的地位の確立に寄与すると期待され、また、日本語教育とタイ語教育の実際の教授技術の向上、教材開発にも大きく貢献する内容である。

第3巻　日本語韓国語の受け身文の対照研究　許明子著　6000円
　　2004年春刊行予定
　　日本語と韓国語の受け身文の対照研究。文法構造と運用面における特徴について分析を行ったもの。第一部では両言語の受け身文の意味的・形態的・構文的な特徴を明らかにすることをめざす。第二部では、話し言葉と書き言葉における受け身文の使い方に関する実態調査に基づいて、語用論的特徴を明らかにする。日本語教育の現場に応用できる指導法および学習法を提案している。

◎＋ゴシックのものは既刊。表示の値段は税抜価格です。その時点での消費税が加算されます。『言語』には毎月、広告をだしておりますので、ご覧ください。また、最新の情報はひつじ書房のホームページに掲載しています。
http://www.hituzi.co.jp/をご覧ください。

2003-7-K

言語学翻訳叢書刊行案内

第1巻　言語普遍性と言語類型論　―統語論と形態論―
　　　バーナード・コムリー著　松本克己・山本秀樹訳　3500円
　　　様々な言語から言語の普遍性と類型論を追究した名著の翻訳。色々なタイプの言語を考察していくことから深められた考察は、日本語を考える際にも有益である。

第2巻　ことばは世界とどうかかわるか　―語用論入門―
　　　ヤコブ・L・メイ著　澤田治美・高司正夫訳　3880円
　　　Journal of Pragmatics誌などのシリーズエディターをつとめている著者の語用論。ユーモアと含蓄に富んだ記述は、話芸といえよう。言語研究のみならず、人文科学全般にも関係のある議論である。

第3巻　ひとは発話をどう理解するか　―関連性理論入門―
　　　ダイアン・ブレイクモア著　武内道子・山崎英一訳　3009円
　　　文化人類学者スペルベルと言語学者ウィルソンによる、人間の認知上の一般原則に基づく伝達理論としての関連性理論の入門書。なぜ人間はわずかな情報だけで発話を理解でき、時に理解に失敗するのか。この日常の会話とアイロニーやメタファーなども統一的に考察できる新しい理論。

第5巻　意味と発話行為
　　　ダニエル・ヴァンダーヴェーケン著　久保進他訳　5000円
　　　言語哲学者サールとも共同研究を行っているヴァンダイヴェーケンによる発話行為理論の決定版。今回の訳者とも共同研究を行っており、翻訳にその成果が生かされている。

第8巻　テクストはどのように構成されるか　―言語の結束性―
　　　M.A.K.ハリディ　ルカイヤ・ハサン著　安藤貞雄他訳　6000円
　　　ことばは次々とつながっていくことで文章や談話になっていく。文の研究から文章の研究へむかいつつある今後の言語研究にとって必須の結束性（cohesion）の基本的文献（原題「Cohesion in English」）。

第9巻　「印欧人」のことば誌　―比較言語学概説―
　　　アンドレ・マルティネ著　神山孝夫訳　3800円
　　　言語学と、歴史学・考古学・文化人類学・宗教学の成果を有機的に関連させて綴る。第Ⅸ～Ⅹ章では著者マルティネが長年温めた印欧祖語についての大胆な構想が展開される。

表示の値段は税抜価格です。その時点での消費税が加算されます。『言語』には毎月、広告をだしておりますので、ご覧ください。また、最新の情報はひつじ書房のホームページに掲載しています。
http://www.hituzi.co.jp/をご覧ください。